THE **NEXT POPE**

Other Books by Peter Hebblethwaite

The Vatican
Pope John XXIII: Shepherd of the Modern World
In the Vatican
Synod Extraordinary
Paul VI: The First Modern Pope
The Year of Three Popes

THE NEXT POPE

*A Behind-the-Scenes Look at the
Forces that Will Choose the Successor
to John Paul II and Decide the Future
of the Catholic Church*

PETER HEBBLETHWAITE

HarperSanFrancisco
A Division of HarperCollins*Publishers*

Photo credits: Catholic News Service for photos on pages 57, 59–62; UPI/ Bettman for photos on page 58.

For information address HarperCollins Publishers, 10 East 53rd Street, New York, NY 10022.

FIRST EDITION
Book design by Ralph Fowler

Library of Congress Cataloging-in-Publication Data
Hebblethwaite, Peter.
The next pope : a behind-the-scenes look at the forces that will choose the successor to John Paul II and decide the future of the Catholic Church / Peter Hebblethwaite. — 1st ed.
p. cm.
Includes bibliographical references and index.
ISBN 0–06–063752–8 (cloth : alk. paper)
1. Popes—History—20th century. 2. Catholic Church. Collegium Cardinalium—History—20th century. 3. John Paul II, Pope, 1920–
4. Catholic Church—History—1965– I. Title.
BX1805.H39 1995   95-1661
262'.135—dc20   CIP

95 96 97 98 99 ❖RRD(H) 10 9 8 7 6 5 4 3 2 1

This edition is printed on acid-free paper that meets the American National Standards Institute Z39.48 Standard.

CONTENTS

A section of photographs begins on page 57

An Action of the Whole Church

Nothing concentrates the mind of the Church so much as a conclave to elect a new pope. And nothing focuses the eyes of the world on Rome and the Vatican so much as a papal election in which the members of the college of cardinals, "the world's most exclusive club," choose the Successor of Saint Peter, the Vicar of Christ on earth. ABC, CNN, CBC, and the world's other TV companies will have their cameras there—outside the walls. Commentators will be reduced to saying, "Behind those walls, history is being made."

The scene in the Sistine Chapel is familiar from movies like *The Cardinal* or the adaptation of Morris West's novel *The Shoes of the Fisherman*. But much of what these films say or imply is out of date. This changeless institution has changed quite a lot. One medieval tradition will not be seen again: The seats where the cardinals sat around the Sistine Chapel were surmounted by canopies serving no known purpose except one. When a pope was elected, all the cardinals downed their canopies, leaving only the new pope with his canopy up. Moreover, conclaves did not happen in the Sistine Chapel until after the collapse of the Papal States in 1870. The next one may well be elsewhere.

The method of voting has changed little for a millennium, however. The rules were devised to prevent cheating. On the tables are ballot papers with the printed formula *Eligo in Summum Pontificem* (I elect as Supreme Pontiff). Below, the cardinals write the name of their first-choice candidate—they are advised to disguise their handwriting so no one can recognize it. This seems rather unnecessary, because the ballot papers are soon going to be burned— the puff of grayish black smoke they provide is the sign to the waiting world that a pope has not been elected. But the scrutineers might recognize the handwriting.

Next, having folded the paper in two, the cardinals advance one by one toward the altar, kneel for a moment in silent prayer, and pronounce the oath: "I call to witness Christ the Lord who will be my judge that my vote is given to the one whom before God I consider should be elected." The cardinal then places the ballot paper on the paten and tips it into the chalice on the altar. It is an awesome act beneath the gaze of Michelangelo's severe, chastising Christ. It stands out in even more alarming and colorful fashion with the grime and candle smoke of centuries cleared away courtesy of the Nippon Television Network Corporation.

The election of a pope in a conclave is one of those in-stitutions of the Catholic world that emerge from the abyss of time immemorial. Yet there is a great contrast between the first and second millenniums. After the Church emerged from the underground in the fourth century, the Bishop of Rome was elected by the parish priests of the city, and the man elected had to be accepted by the populace. In 1059 Pope Nicholas II restricted the electoral college to cardi-nals—at that date an unscriptural novelty of recent devising. But to this day each new cardinal is assigned a church in Rome of which he is the notional pastor. So Cardinal Basil Hume of Westminster in London had to "take possession" of the church of San Silvestro in downtown Rome before truly belonging to the college of cardinals.

There is another contrast between the conclaves of the Middle Ages and those of the last two centuries. In the late Middle Ages, the college of cardinals was a tightly-knit group mostly of Italians who deliberately wanted to be small in number so as not to dilute their power. In 1517 Leo X (the Medici pope who said, "Now we have the pa-pacy, let us at least enjoy it") executed one cardinal, impris-oned several others, and packed the college with thirty-one place-hunters. It was not the "cause" of the Reformation, but it helped. In 1586, the post-Tridentine pope Sixtus V fixed the number of cardinals at not more than seventy. We had to wait until Pope John XXIII in 1958 for that rule to be breached.

After Vatican II (1962–65), the council summoned un-expectedly, indeed, astonishingly, by Pope John XXIII, the idea of restricting the papal election to the college of cardinals seemed anomalous in a Church that now saw itself as the People of God on its pilgrim march through history. In the era of collegiality too many voices were excluded from the conclave—the voices of the local churches from four continents, of women, of the young or even the middle-aged, and above all, of the poor, all are shut out. Paul VI wanted to change radically the arrangements for the conclave, made a brave start, and then drew back in alarm at what he had done.

He excluded the over-eighties—an incredibly controversial move, for the over-eighties at least. On Italian television, Cardinal Eugène Tisserant fumed, while Cardinal Alfredo Ottaviani's jowls wobbled with indignation. What Paul VI did, in effect, was declare that being a cardinal did not carry with it a prescriptive *right* to elect the pope. It was a small change. But a small change is as important in principle as a big one: a future pope could realize Paul's VI's original plan and, say, make the presidents of episcopal colleges the electoral college, whether they were cardinals or not.

Though this has not yet happened, something of the collegial mode of thinking inspired by Vatican II remains. Sometime in the third millennium one must expect the rules to be changed to reflect this. "It takes fifty to a hundred years for councils to have their effect," is the common judgment of Church historians. In any case, Paul VI envisaged the whole Church as somehow engaged or participating in a conclave—if only by prayer. He pictured the scene in the Acts of the Apostles where Mary, the mother of Jesus, is present among the disciples, and "the whole gathering/church persevered in prayer with one heart" (Acts 1:14). He goes on, "Thus the election of the new pope will not be an event isolated from the People of God which concerns only the electoral college, but, in a certain sense, it will be an action of the whole Church" (*Romano Pontifice Eligendo*, no. 85).

It is surely difficult to perceive the link between the gathering of terrified disciples in the upper room with Mary and, indeed, many other women in their midst and a papal conclave, just as it is hard to grasp the link between the Last Supper and Pontifical High Mass with clouds of billowing incense. Yet that is what Catholics have to do: discover their Christian and biblical origins.

Very instructive for conclave history is a book that appeared in 1877, while Pio Nono (as Pius IX was always known in the English-speaking world) was still reigning. When Ruggiero Bonghi published his *Pio Nono e il Papa futuro (Pius IX and the Future Pope)*, he was of course unaware that he was writing just one year before the death of Pio Nono. It was already the longest papacy in history, having lasted thirty-one years at that date. Perhaps that gives us a subsidiary law: don't appoint a young pope, or he will be around forever. Pio Nono was forty-six when elected; John Paul II was fifty-eight. Conventional wisdom said they were both much too young.

Back, however, to Bonghi in 1877. With unerring precision he predicted that the next pope would be the archbishop of Perugia, Cardinal Gioacchino Pecci. How did he

justify this? Quite simply on the grounds that Pecci represented an *alternative* to Pio Nono in every respect.

Cardinal Pecci had stood aloof from the pontificate for
the most part. He had set up an alternative court in Perugia,
patronized learning and the arts, and written pastoral letters
that had the sweep and scope of encyclicals, for which they
were dress rehearsals. No one else had done this so manifestly. No one else was a candidate. Of course, one can say
that Bonghi's task was made easier by the length of Pio
Nono's pontificate: the idea of an alternative, a radical
change, was in the air, for by this time Pio Nono was unpopular in Italy.

Nothing new in that. All popes tend to grow in unpopularity toward the end of their reign; and the longer they last,
the more unpopular they become and the more they stand
in the way of necessary change, becoming obstacles to re-
sponsiveness to the needs of the Church and the world.

I do not claim to emulate Bonghi. There is no Pecci
around today, though Cardinal Carlo Maria Martini, the
Jesuit from Milan, has features in common with him. The
first time I met him, he made a remark apropos of something I had written about CCEE (Concilium Conferentiarum Episcopatum Europearum, or Council of European
Episcopal Conferences), of which he was president in succession to Cardinal Basil Hume: "You seem to have a good
understanding of the way my mind works." I looked modestly at the ground, waiting for the inevitable "but." "But,"
he went on, "there is just one thing wrong." I wondered
what it might be. "You are much too kind to me," he said. I
promised to do better in future.

There was in 1877 one obvious objection to Bonghi's theory of the need for an alternative pope: all the cardinals who would meet in the conclave to elect Pio Nono's successor had been "created"—the technical term—by the man himself; and it had to be presumed that they shared in his pessimistic, defensive view of the world. But—and this is another conclave law—however loyal cardinals may be to the pope who created them, they are not his creatures, and they are in any case liberated by his death, freed to make a fresh start.

Besides, most cardinals know they are likely to experience only one conclave in their lives. They have enough sense of responsibility to wish to bring the voices of the young and the poor with them into the conclave. And they have enough conscience genuinely to ask themselves what the Spirit is saying to the Church today. If that law operated in 1878, why should it not operate in 199x?

ONE The Next Conclave

Popes are elected for life, and there is no such thing as a deputy pope. Consequently, no one is "a heartbeat away from the papacy." Yet someone has to take charge when the pope dies. In 1991 Spanish Cardinal Eduardo Martinez Somalo was appointed *camerlengo*, or chamberlain. His first task will be to check that John Paul II is truly dead by tapping him on the forehead with a silver hammer.

Then he has to organize the funeral, to which world statesmen will come—Mikhail Gorbachev will be in the front row, and Saddam Hussein might invite himself. Then he must arrange for the *Novemdiales*, or nine days of mourning during which cardinals will praise the recently deceased pope, and delicately hint at *what sort of pope* should succeed him. But Martinez Somalo's main task is to organize the conclave to elect the next pope. The one certainty is that he won't be elected himself.

The assembly of cardinals that will elect Pope John Paul's successor is called a conclave because they will be locked up *conclave* (with a key) inside the apostolic palace to the right of St. Peter's. Telephone wires will be ripped out; outward-looking windows will be shuttered and sealed. The cardinals will be searched to see that they have not brought in mobile phones, modems, fax machines, or bugging devices. They will be incommunicado and uncomfortable, lodged in improvised accommodations with rudimentary facilities. Hundreds of journalists and television reporters will converge upon Rome. For many, the Vatican will be a fresh assignment and a new experience. Much nonsense will be written. Bookmakers will offer odds. Fools will take them.

Yet, a few things may be said with fair certainty about this future event. The conclave will be made up of a maximum of 120 cardinals, none of whom will be over eighty. Although the cardinals could theoretically elect any male Catholic, the chances are that the next pope will be sitting there among them. So it is safe to assume that the next pope will be male and will emerge from the college of cardinals. According to the predictions customarily ascribed to the twelfth-century archbishop of Armagh, Saint Malachy, his motto will be *Oliva pacis*—The olive branch of peace.

Beyond that, it is impossible to predict the result of the next conclave, for the simple reason that we do not know *when* it will occur. If Pope John Paul reaches the age of eighty—as have the majority of popes in this century—he will still be around in 2000. By then, he would most certainly have appointed more cardinals, who would further alter the composition of the electoral college. He clearly *hopes* to be around in 2000. The year of the millennium fascinates him like the eye of the basilisk. His first encyclical, *Redemptor Hominis*, already looked forward to it. The decade of evangelization is designed to prepare for it. He called a special meeting of cardinals in mid-1994 to decide how to celebrate it.

So John Paul would dearly like to reach the year 2000. By 1994 John Paul II was in the sixteenth year of his pontificate. Undoubtedly we have entered the *preconclave* period that comes toward the end of any long pontificate. This can be said without having any privileged insight into the state of Pope John Paul's health. The two operations he underwent in 1981 for the removal of the bullets of the Turkish assassin who tried to kill him in St. Peter's Square on May 13, feast of Our Lady of Fátima, would have taxed the strength of a less tough constitution.

But he recovered, remarkably, attributing his escape to Our Lady of Fátima. On the first anniversary of the shooting, in 1982, he went to Fátima in Portugal and left behind one of the bullets as a memento. He was back again in 1991 on the tenth anniversary of the shooting. On his return to Rome he remarked, "I consider this entire decade to be a free gift, given to me in a special way by Divine Providence."[1] So he has a sense of living on borrowed time, and feels confirmed in his policies: if he has been spared by Divine Providence, it is surely for some purpose.

Eleven years after the failed assassination attempt, on July 15, 1992, there was another health scare. John Paul underwent an operation for the removal of a tumor of the colon "about the size of an orange." It was reassuring to learn that it was a "benign growth," less so to realize that it had not been diagnosed earlier. But the Vatican press office would allow no word of criticism of the papal doctor, Dr. Renato Buzzonetti, and the press officer, Joaquín Navarro-Valls, insisted early in 1993 that the pope was fine:

> *I would say that he is more healthy than before. He has scars on his intestine which were removed along with the tumor. Now he is able to digest his food well. . . . The July 15 operation was definitive; there won't be another one. Three biopsies were done, before, during and after the operation. And there is something more: on January 18, 1993, the Holy Father underwent a complete check-up. All the tests gave results with the normal range.*

He pointed to the full and exhausting program of visits to Africa—including the politically delicate Sudan—to Albania and in June to Spain as evidence of rude health.

Pope John Paul's state of health soon became the subject of Roman jokes—with the pope himself as the leading joker. After addressing the United Nations Food and Agriculture Organization on Sunday, November 14, 1993, he moved to his right, but an aide called him the other way and he missed a step, falling heavily on his right shoulder and dislocating it. He got up unaided, paused for a moment, and then continued to shake hands and bless with his left hand. There had been no blackout. A night in the Gemelli Hospital put his right shoulder back in place.

The next time he appeared in public, Saturday, November 20, 1993, his right arm was hidden by a sling beneath his crimson cape so that, he quipped, "the photographers cannot immortalize this deficient pope and show him to the world." "But you have a right to see it, a right to see it," he went on, "thus paying tribute to the mass media," enthused one optimistic commentator. John Paul made a mistake in Italian (though some claimed he did it on purpose). He kept using the word *deficiente* as though he thought it meant physically weak; in fact, it means mentally disadvantaged. As soon as he sat down on his throne in the Nervi audience hall for the meeting with health workers organized by Cardinal Fiorenzo Angelini, he declared, "As you can see, the pope is a bit *deficiente*—but he's not finished yet." Mild titters. "The deficient pope greets all of you," he plunged on, "but he's not yet in a state of collapse [*decaduto*]." More laughter.

Being a polyglot has its disadvantages. In Colombia, John Paul was asked what he most enjoyed eating during his stay there. "*El hombre,*" he cannibalistically replied, thinking the question was about what he had most enjoyed, period.

Marco Politi of *La Repubblica* contrived an interview with Dr. Corrado Manni, chief anesthetist at Rome's Gemelli Hospital, that gave a more serious view of John Paul's health. On the plane to Denver in August 1993 Politi noticed that John Paul's left hand was constantly trembling.

He tried to disguise this by holding it steady with his right hand or, when seated, by leaning on his left hand with his head characteristically on one side. Now that his left hand had to do all the work, it was harder to conceal the trembling.

What was the significance of this? Politi asked. Manni replied, "There could be lots of causes. There could for example be neurological reasons. Or there could be a slight trembling in moments of special stress. But it cannot in any case be related to the tumor that has been cleared up. There could be many different causes. In another person—I stress in another person—Parkinson's disease could begin like that." Despite the cautious formulation, both Manni and Politi got into hot water with the Vatican press office for this remark.

Manni's explanation for the fact that John Paul often seems listless in the morning and then brightens up in the course of the day was that "he leads an infernal life, getting up at 5:30 in the morning, and working a seventeen-hour day." The pope is strong as an ox, said Manni, but with the years and the overwork he has imposed on himself, "there are bound to be signs of tiredness." In Manni's opinion the pope should try to lead a quieter life. He had once said, "Holy Father, couldn't you work a little less?" To which the pope replied with astonishment, "you mean, *still less?*" In his own mind, he has already made enough concessions to his medical advisers.

But then, just three weeks before his seventy-fourth birthday—on May 18, 1994—he slipped and fell getting out of his bath at 11 P.M. on Thursday, April 28. Dr. Renato Buzzonetti was soon on the scene. An X-ray examination revealed that John Paul had broken his right femur (thigh bone). A mild sedative enabled him to sleep through the night; it was thought he would be better prepared for surgery if he were properly rested. Next morning at 10 A.M. he was taken to the Gemelli Hospital. He is getting to know the place well: this was his sixth stay there. The official medical bulletin, signed by four physicians, said simply, "Tests given at the hospital confirmed the earlier diagnosis of a fracture of the right femur. The pope then underwent surgery for arthro-prosthesis. The operation lasted about two hours." It was all very formal. Gianfranco Fineschi, who performed the surgery, attempted a joke: "From now on the pope will not have the hip that God made but one a bioengineer made."

Back in the Vatican press office, Joaquín Navarro-Valls, whose medical qualifications ensure a good command of technical vocabulary, insisted that the pope's general health remained good. He "absolutely excluded the possibility of the pope's losing consciousness or feeling sick, either before or after the fall."

In other words, the fall was an accident, such as might happen to anyone in bare feet on those slippery Roman marble floors. But this time there were graver consequences. The pope will never ski again, never climb another mountain, and may be hindered in walking.

So the bulletins continued to be, on the whole, reassuring. Yet the preconclave atmosphere was felt within the

Vatican itself even more intensely. Healthy though he may be, the pope is not immortal. Leo XIII, who just made it into this century, died in 1903 at the age of ninety-three. His lengthy reign led a cardinal to remark, "We elected a Holy Father, not an eternal father." Such longevity in popes cannot be taken for granted. Even the most sanguine would not expect John Paul to be still around in the year 2013.

Of course, the reason Vatican officials insist so much on the pope's splendid state of health is that they do not wish to give the impression that the pontificate is practically over or that it has entered a lame-duck phase.

Yet it was hard to think of anything that remained for John Paul to do. There are various cutoff points at which, had he died, one could have said that he had achieved much. In 1983 he promulgated the new code of canon law. In 1985 he celebrated, in his own way, the twenty-fifth anniversary of Vatican II. In 1991, in the Synod on Europe, he welcomed the collapse of Communism, to which he had undoubtedly contributed importantly. The next year, 1992, saw the publication of *The Catechism of the Catholic Church* in Italy and France. It came out in Britain and the United States in mid-1994, after translation difficulties about "inclusive language."

However, the pope still had something up his sleeve. He had first a formidable encyclical called *Veritatis Splendor,* leaked in late July 1992, which formulated the basic principles of Catholic moral theology and demanded disciplinary action against moral theologians who "dissented."

So Pope John Paul still thought, late in 1993, not only that he had something more to do, but that it was extremely important and urgent. For the point about *Veritatis Splendor* is that it is aimed not just at sporadic or occasional "dissent" from Catholic moral teaching from people who cannot follow, say, the official line on contraception or homosexuality but against "an overall and systematic calling into question of traditional moral doctrine" (4). If true, this would be a very serious matter. The pope believes that a "secularized culture" has invaded the Church (88). Writing out of a deep sense of *crisis*, the pope warns against "dissent in the form of carefully orchestrated protests and polemics carried on in the media" (113). He exhorts bishops, to whom the encyclical is addressed, to take "appropriate measures to ensure that the faithful are guarded from every theory and doctrine" contrary to the Church's moral teaching (116).

But this was not his last word on the subject. *Veritatis Splendor* was about morality in general. The next encyclical will be on morality in particular, and will be a pro-life treatise. John Paul announced it October 9, 1994, at a Mass celebrating the Year of the Family: "God willing at the close of this year [that is, the Year of the Family], as one of its most precious fruits and as a program for the future, I will publish the already announced encyclical on life." That is what his prepared text said. What he actually said differed only in the last clause: "I will *try* to publish . . ."

Veritatis Splendor and its putative successor have some bearing on the next conclave. For there are cardinals who do not share the pope's sense of alarm and crisis and therefore are unsympathetic toward its disciplinary conclusions. Cardinal Basil Hume of Westminster, while praising Pope John Paul's attack on "moral relativism" (that was the easy part), averred that "there is nothing new here." Relations with moral theologians in England and Wales were good, he explained. He said, in effect, Crisis? What crisis? In explaining *Veritatis Splendor,* Cardinal Basil Hume explained it away. Like a skillful conjuror, his sleight of hand made the encyclical vanish in a puff of verbiage.

But clearly, the pope would not have written his encyclical unless he sincerely believed there was a serious crisis. In any event, it proved that he felt there was still work to be done, made all the more urgent because his pontificate is in its final phase.

There was other unfinished business of a disciplinary nature. Men and women religious were also to be called to order in the synod devoted to them in 1994. It was anticipated with some gloom. Sister Helena O'Donaghue, general of the Killaloe branch of the Mercy Sisters, said, "I feel that the draft *Lineamenta* [or preparatory documents] present a vision of consecrated life as a kind of package, staid and static, seen through a narrow lens and described in sawdust language."[2]

In fact the synod turned out to be much better than feared. Under Cardinal Basil Hume's astute presidency, religious men and women, standing shoulder to shoulder, managed to assert their prophetic vocation and international role. "Think globally, act locally," was their slogan.

The reactions to *Veritatis Splendor* and the Synod on the Consecrated Life are evidence of a widespread feeling of malaise: the pontificate is malfunctioning. For all the intense and incessant activity, the voluminous flow of encyclicals and instructions, the endless globe-trotting, the pontificate is to some extent whirling away in a void, cut off from the real life of the People of God. The disappointing answer to the question, What more is there for this pontificate to do? is, Yet more of the same.

The historic "first" of October 19, 1994, did nothing to dispel that impression. John Paul became the first pope to write a book while sitting in Peter's chair. *Crossing the Threshold of Hope* certainly crossed the frontiers of hype.[3] It told us nothing we did not know already. John Paul appears as a friendly old professor of, say, comparative linguistics and philosophy whose reading was a long time ago. The reader wishing to discover the "bleak picture" of contemporary humanity is advised to "consider Fyodor Dostoevsky, Franz Kafka, or Albert Camus."[4] The book was presented as "a conversation with ordinary families in their homes."

What will ordinary folk make of this? "In addition it is not possible to affirm that when something is transempirical it ceases to be empirical."[5]

We must always allow for what Cardinal Léon-Joseph Suenens calls "the surprises of the Holy Spirit." But what is *surprising* is precisely what is not predicted or predictable. It now seems highly unlikely, in human terms, that there could be any new directions in the present pontificate. Popes, like most people, get more conservative with old age. It is the next conclave, and only the next conclave, that can provide "a surprise of the Holy Spirit."

Such talk is anathema in Rome. The emphasis on the blooming health and activism of Pope John Paul is also designed to quash rumors about his possible resignation. There are not many precedents. Four popes abdicated: Clement I, number three after Peter, in 97; Pontian, in 235, to allow a successor to take over when he was carted off to Sardinia and the mines; Benedict IX, in 1045 (though he made a comeback); and Celestine V, in 1294, the last pope to resign.[6] All except Benedict were canonized.

Paul VI went to visit Saint Celestine's tomb at Anagni in 1966. Everyone thought—wrongly, as it turned out—that he was hinting at his own imminent resignation when he said, "After a few months Saint Celestine understood that he was being deceived by those who surrounded him." John Paul does not have that reason for resigning. Those who surround him would be hard pressed to deceive him. He is manifestly in charge. Nor need he expect to be unseated, deposed, as were seven of his predecessors between 537 and 1048.

But there is a new factor since the Council. The Church is less of a gerontocracy than it was as recently as the 1950s. This is due to two reforms introduced by Paul VI. The retirement age for cardinals is eighty, and the over-eighties cannot take part in the conclave. Bishops must tender their resignation to the pope when they reach seventy-five.

It would not be unreasonable to imagine a Bishop of Rome retiring at eighty—if the over-eighties are incapable of electing a pope, how can one of their number do the job?—and to think of resigning at seventy-five.

Jean Chélini, a French historian close to the late Cardinal Jacques Martin, hinted as long ago as 1984 that Pope John Paul had considered a certain "scenario of resignation." He concludes his book *Au Vatican de Jean-Paul II* thus:

> *Certain intimates of Pope John Paul II give one to understand [*laissent entendre*] that he will retire at seventy-five and, after a "sportive" sabbatical year, would retire to the Carmelite convent he wanted to enter as a young student. Is it this prospect that makes John Paul so serene, so cheerful, like a man who is certain about the future?*[7]

"Sportive" for a seventy-five-year-old presumably meant a little gentle skiing or mountaineering. But though resignation might have been contemplated in 1984, theoretically at least, it seems much less likely as the reality of the seventy-fifth birthday draws closer. No quitter, Pope John Paul intends to die in harness.

But he won't go on forever. On his return home in 1991, his Polish fans greeted him with the traditional chant *Sto Lat!* (May you live to be a hundred years!). In reply he quipped, "If this pope lives all those years, your grandchildren will be coming to see him, and what could be done with such an old pope? I can see only one solution: he'll have to run away and live in a monastery." That echoes the Chélini hypothesis.

Sound papal health and no prospect of resignation or deposition. Yet these factors still cannot dispel the preconclave mood, and, obviously, the feeling will intensify the

longer the pontificate grinds on. Nor can one say that speculation about the succession is confined to "irresponsible
journalists." It is the stuff of private conversations in the
Curia, whose members read the works of the "irresponsible
journalists" with knowing winks and dismissive shrugs.

Here is an example from my own experience. In an article published originally in the *Irish Times* and the *National
Catholic Reporter* in September 1992, I offered a classic list
of three names (a *terna*). I stressed that these were not predictions, said that everything depended on the timing, and
confessed that I had not the faintest idea who would be the
next pope. But if there were a conclave *fairly soon*, I carefully explained, these were the names that sprang to mind.

I began with Cardinal Carlo Maria Martini, archbishop
of Milan, as the best equipped, intellectually and spiritually, to succeed. Objection: he is a Jesuit, and not only has
there never been a Jesuit pope, there has never before been
a Jesuit cardinal who was a serious candidate for the papacy.
Next came Cardinal Pio Laghi, former nuncio in Argentina
and the United States, who was said by good sources to be
"the candidate of the United States cardinals." Objection:
he is intellectually lightweight and (born May 22, 1922) is
only two years younger than Pope John Paul. His chances
diminish the longer the pontificate goes on.

But it was my third long shot, the dark horse, that
aroused most interest. For a Third-World candidate I proposed Nigerian cardinal Francis J. Arinze, president since
1984 of the Council for Inter-religious Dialogue. As such, he
has been responsible for dialogue with Muslims who form

half the population of Nigeria. He has had very good relations with them. He has shown himself capable of running a Roman office—though a small one—and proved a good talent spotter, an essential attribute for a pope.

If the great achievement of John Paul II is to have "dealt with" Communism, then undoubtedly the next challenging task for the papacy will be dealing with Islam. For that, Cardinal Arinze is better equipped than anyone else. And he is black: that would strike the imagination of the world, just as the "Polishness" of Karol Wojtyla captured it in 1978.

The point of this story is what happened next. Two months later I met the secretary of the Council for Interreligious Dialogue, British Missionary of Africa (formerly White Fathers) Michael Fitzgerald. He looked very severe, said that I had behaved very badly and irresponsibly and had caused "great difficulties" to his cardinal, who was "very displeased." What difficulties? I inquired. After all, though calumny and detraction are to be avoided, it is not injurious to someone's reputation to suggest that he could conceivably be elected pope. But that was not the point. Apparently, some people were too scared to invite Cardinal Arinze henceforward, on the grounds that they might seem to be "currying favor" with the "next pope." An awkwardness was introduced into relationships.

Of course what had happened was that my highly tentative, carefully guarded, nuanced remarks had become virtual certainties by the time they reached Nigeria. Prestigious newspapers in Europe and America had headlines stating NIGERIAN NEXT POPE. The Muslim papers took it up enthusiastically, especially, of course, in Nigeria. This cautionary tale has another lesson. Although Cardinal Arinze was "displeased," he began tut-tutting only after he had time to think about it and adjust his attitudes; his immediate reaction had been one of pleasure that someone had thought of him. "Ibos are never lacking in self-confidence," said the source.

It should be now clear that I do not propose to embark on foolish predictions about the next pope. That is not the point, not at all. A conclave throws the spotlight on the Vatican in a way nothing else does. For a few weeks the college of cardinals is scrutinized with great intensity. Nothing is as much fun as an unpredictable election. But it is also an opportunity to ask where the Church stands. It raises the fundamental questions: "What sort of pope do we need in what sort of Church for what sort of World?"[8]

Of course it is the college of cardinals, and the college of cardinals alone, that actually has to decide whom to elect on the basis of these discussions. But they are not, and would not wish to be, sundered from the rest of the Church. They carry the whole Church with them in their deliberations.

Nor can it be said that speculation about the succession is confined to irresponsible journalists. Cardinal Achille Silvestrini, prefect of the Congregation for the Oriental Churches, born October 25, 1923, will be present at any conclave occurring before 2003. He is the first cardinal publicly to share his thoughts on the subject—without, of course, giving any names. He could be a key figure.

In an interview published in the Italian geopolitical review *Limes*, Cardinal Silvestrini recalled that all popes in the nineteenth century came from the Papal States, over which, up till 1870, they were the temporal as well as the spiritual rulers. In the twentieth century, the circle widened to include anyone born in Italy. Three were patriarchs of Venice: Saint Pius X, John XXIII, and John Paul I. Two were archbishops of Milan: Pius XI and Paul VI. Benedict XV came from Bologna, and Pius XII, the only Roman-born pope of the century, was in the Curia as cardinal secretary of state under his predecessor Pius XI.

Cardinal Silvestrini maintained that with the election of a Polish pope, John Paul II, in October 1978, the geographical boundaries have been overcome and "anything becomes possible." The next pope would be chosen, he suggested, not on grounds of nationality but on grounds of personality: "In the future, who knows? It could well be that a Latin American or an African would emerge."[9] This corresponded to a widespread feeling that "no one is a foreigner in Rome." The universal Church is not bedeviled by narrow nationalism. John Paul II having broken through the nationality barrier, the next conclave will be the most open ever.

However, Cardinal Silvestrini's remarks may be considered obvious: their main interest is that they show a cardinal who is actively thinking about the next conclave. If *his* thoughts run along these lines, then others cardinals may well have had similar thoughts—but they keep them to themselves.

In two respects, however, Cardinal Silvestrini's remarks omit some vital elements. The cardinals meet in conclave to elect the Bishop of Rome, the successor of Saint Peter, and this is foundation of all his grander titles: Primate of Italy, Patriarch of the West, Pontiff of the Universal Church. Rome needs a bishop. It is therefore arguable that the next pope should be, if not an Italian, then at least an Italian-speaker. A pope who could not address the crowd in St. Peter's Square in their own language is almost inconceivable. If true, that narrows the field—though perhaps not by very much. It would exclude most North American cardinals, for a start.

The second flaw in Cardinal Silvestrini's argument lies in his emphasis on the *personality* of the candidate. John Paul II overcame the obstacle of his Polishness, he says, because those who knew him and heard him speak recognized "his unique personality and charisma," and regarded him as a "father of the Church" for his fervor and doctrine. No doubt this contains an aspect of the truth. But conclaves are not in the habit of electing the most charismatic personality available. The next two chapters will illustrate this.

However John Paul II came to be elected pope on October 16, 1978, he certainly looked like a new sort of pope: young, athletic, endlessly talented as linguist and philosopher of international repute, the first non-Italian since the unfortunate Hadrian VI, who died in 1523, allegedly poisoned by his Roman doctor, who could not stand his reforming ways. The cynical Romans put up a statue to the papal doctor.

John Paul II did not have to fear, at this stage, his doctors. But on May 13, 1981, Mehmet Ali Agca, a Turkish "Gray Wolf" who had already killed twice, shot him in St. Peter's Square. Cardinal Basil Hume, imagining that the pope might be an invalid from now on, suggested that this would lead to a new form of pontificate, a suffering pope pinned to his bed of pain like common humanity: "It is possible that a new kind of apostolate is now open to this ardent man. He has had his fill of mass meetings, and it could be said that the transient fervor of these occasions seems hardly relevant to the condition of humanity today."[10]

It would be difficult to get him more wrong. Far from having had his fill of mass meetings, John Paul II went on to have as many of them as possible, totting up his sixty-second international journey by September 1994. He seemed positively to enjoy what Cardinal Hume called the "transient fervor" of crowds.

The most recent evidence suggests that the May 13, 1981, assassination attempt was not the result of a KGB plot, exploiting DIGOS, the Bulgarian secret service. Rather, the CIA successfully *pinned* the freelance efforts of a lapsed Muslim on DIGOS, and therefore the KGB. But to accept that would spoil the story of fiendish Soviet Communists versus lily-white American democrats.

So if the failed assassination attempt confirmed John Paul in the wisdom of his policies and their providential underpinning, what consequences did this have? The principal consequence was that he no longer needed to listen to any advice within the Church and could concentrate on his personal agenda. Pope John Paul II was not the first pope to have ruled the Church from the extreme right—Pope Saint Pius X did the same—but he was the first post–Vatican II pope to attempt this tour de force.

It is manifestly impossible to write a book about a future event. But this fact does not condemn one to silence, for one can still prepare for the event, make it understandable in advance, and outline the issues it will have to face. Throughout, a very fundamental question is being asked: Whom are the cardinals electing? It may seem obvious to say that they are electing a pope. But in the early Church (and still in the Orthodox churches) *pope* merely means father, and it was applied to all priests. The Copts of Egypt call their patriarch "pope." In any case *pope* has no theological content, and the term is never used in conciliar documents. Vatican Council I speaks, grandly, of the Roman Pontiff, or *Pontifex Romanus* (the bridge builder), a title that takes us back to the Roman emperors.

A much more fundamental title is Bishop of Rome. The cardinals, notionally the parish priests of Rome, are electing their bishop, and not merely in a notional sense. Pius XII (1939–58) had such an exalted view of "sacred Rome" (the *sacra città)* that he was unable to pay much attention to his diocese. He sacralized Rome to make it the heart and center of the universal Church of which he was the universal pastor. He rarely emerged from the Vatican (except to console the victims of the air raid on San Lorenzo in July 1943). Roman-born though he was, he seemed to regard the diocese as little more than his point of insertion into the wider world.

Pope John XXIII (1958–63) had a different view. He made a point of *acting* as the Bishop of Rome because Rome *needed* a bishop. He regarded Rome, said Giuseppe Alberigo, "as his own Church, the one for whose salvation he was responsible, the first guarantee of everything else he did."[11] Pope John was not just a theoretical Bishop of Rome: he visited its prisons, its hospitals, and above all, its parishes. He made much of his "taking possession" of St. John Lateran, his true cathedral (the basilica of St. Peter's belongs to the whole Church), and thought of moving his office there.

So the cardinals are electing, in the first place, a Bishop of Rome. That has consequences, as a glance at history will show.

TWO **Learning from the Past**

In this chapter we will look at conclaves of roughly the last two centuries to see what lessons can be learned. But there is one more thing that can be said for certain about the next pope: he will be the 265th successor of Saint Peter—give or take some obscure or doubtful candidates.

Do the origins of the popes conform to any cultural or geographical pattern? The following table summarizes their background:

Origin	as percent of 264
Rome	37.5
Italy (minus Rome)	40.9
Greece/Asia Minor	6.8
Africa	1.1
Europe (minus Italy)	12.5 (6.4 French)
Other (and unknown)	1.2.[1]

A few comments on this table. If we add together the Romans and the Italians (using the term for the peninsula), we reach 78.4 percent, a not unreasonable figure for the Bishop of Rome.

The "Greek" period of dominance is crammed into the years between 654 and 752, when eight out of seventeen popes came from the Middle East, mostly Syrian monks driven westward by the onslaught of Islam. The 6.4 percent French popes also fall within a narrow time band, between 999 and 1378, when there were seventeen of them. Seven of the French popes came between 1305 and 1378, the result of the "Gallican" policies of Philippe le Bel, who installed the papacy firmly at Avignon in France.

There were only three "Germans," three Spaniards, and one Englishman, Nicholas Breakspear, who became Adrian IV (1154–59). Born in Abbots Langley, near St. Albans, son of a humble clerk who later became a monk of St. Albans, Breakspear made his name as a diplomat in Scandinavia. A friend of the political philosopher John of Salisbury, who thought Thomas Becket could have been more accommodating and witnessed his murder in Canterbury cathedral, Breakspear was said to be able to accept criticism. It was in his pontificate, however, that the possibly blasphemous title "Vicar of Christ" first became common.

The Irish remember him as the man who blessed Henry II's attempt to incorporate Ireland in his kingdom—so much for the last and only English pope. The last non-Italian was Adrian VI (1522–23). Between him and John Paul II was a gap of 455 years.

Not for nothing is the phrase "We think in centuries here" a favorite in the Vatican. But, as already stated, in the first millennium, popes did not emerge from the college of cardinals, because cardinals in the modern sense did not yet exist. "By the beginning of the twelfth century," writes John F. Brodrick, S.J., "the entire sacred college acted as the elective body for the selection of Roman Pontiffs. Official recognition of this practice came in 1179 at Lateran Council III in the decree *Licet de evitanda*. Ever since then the college has retained this enormous power."[2]

If we take 1179 as a conservative starting point for the history of conclaves, that gives us ninety-four conclaves to analyze. The medieval and Renaissance ones cannot be dealt with here; the last two hundred years will provide enough material for reflection and instruction. The first rule is that all conclaves are the same, yet each one is different. Certain patterns recur; some lessons—one cannot call them laws—emerge. But nearly every time there is a new factor.

The "Catholic powers" of Europe took a great interest in who was pope because the pope was also a temporal sovereign, the ruler of the Papal States. They ordered their ambassadors to veto (the right of "exclusion") unsound candidates and intrigue for their own favorites. A conclave was a highly political event. François-René de Chateaubriand, the man whose book *Le Génie du Christianisme* made religion fashionable again after the French Revolution, intrigued for France. He wanted a liberal pope.[3] All this offstage activity meant that rigorous secrecy was impossible to maintain.

Antonio Rosmini, founder of the Rosminians and author of *The Five Wounds of the Church*, reported the latest gossip to the bishop of Trent, which was then part of Austria:

> *The conclave is this time being held at the Quirinal. The Cardinals left the church of San Silvestro on foot and the* Veni Creator *was sung among an immense concourse of people. . . . Three more cardinals went in yesterday [making forty in all]. Our cardinals are there, that is the Hungarian and one from Milan, but not the Archduke Rudolph and the French Cardinals. I do not think the Spanish and Portuguese will come, partly because they are too old and partly because they are too busy.*
>
> *In the first scrutinies it is stated as a fact that Cardinal Pacca had twenty votes: He only needed five more for two-thirds.*
>
> *M. de Chateaubriand said he wanted Cardinal Pacca excluded, but this appears to have been a private bombshell for he had not yet received his credentials from the court to the Sacred College. Nothing is known of the scrutinies that followed, but it seems that Pacca is out of the running. This cardinal has the reputation of great piety, of being a good theologian and a good administrator, but he is supposed to be too gentle and easy to influence. He gained a great reputation during the persecution of Pius VII. As Pacca's supporters have not succeeded, it is thought that the Conclave will be somewhat prolonged.*[4]

Rosmini was right about that. The conclave ran from February 23 to March 31, being further delayed by the late arrival of Cardinal Albani, who held the "veto" of the Austrian emperor. The veto, in effect, the right to blackball certain candidates, meant that the conclave was not "free." However, stretching a point, it could be said to represent the last vestige of "lay involvement" in the process of choosing a pope.

In 1829 the result was that a compromise candidate, Cardinal Francesco Saverio Castiglioni, was elected and took the name Pius VIII. But he was sixty-eight and in such bad health that he was unable to celebrate the liturgy in public. He lasted only twenty months, dying in 1830 as revolution broke out in France, Poland, and Hungary and the Papal States.

MORAL: Don't elect a sick pope.

The 1830 conclave was conditioned by this political situation. The Austrian statesman Klemens von Metternich wanted a strong pope who would not "give way to the madness of the age." He found his man in Bartolomeo Alberto Cappellari, author in 1799 of a courageously *unpolitically* correct book called *The Triumph of the Holy See and the Church Against the Attacks of Innovators*. A Camaldolese monk, he took the name Gregory XVI partly in memory of his twenty years as abbot of San Gregorio on the Coelian Hill. From this abbey, Gregory the Great dispatched Augustine to Canterbury and England in 596. Gregory XVI had a more immediate link with England in that he knew the Italian Passionist Dominic Barberi, who received John Henry Newman into the Church in 1845, and Nicholas Wiseman, who in 1850 became the first archbishop of Westminster.

But the conclave lasted fifty days and was very onerous. This time the Spanish veto worked against Cardinal Giustiniani, who was related to the English Catholic aristocracy via the Clifford and the Weld families. As in 1829, Cardinal Albani led the intrigues: an intercepted note showed him to be working against Cappellari, and his candidate, Macchi, stalled at twelve votes. Cappellari became pope. He gave Albani and Metternich every satisfaction on the ideological front.

MORAL: Don't elect a pope on the basis of his writings, and don't elect a theologian—he will be unable to leave theology to others.

Thus we reach June 1846, when Pius IX (invariably known as Pio Nono thanks to Mr. Gladstone[5]) began the longest pontificate history has ever known—thirty-two years. It brought to an end the series of conclaves held in the centuries-old lifetime of the Papal States. For the last time the fifty out of sixty-two cardinals who came to Rome (twelve invalids or slowpokes did not make it) were electing not just the Bishop of Rome but the temporal sovereign of the Papal States. The Papal States, already embryonically present when Gregory the Great sent Saint Augustine to England in 596, by the nineteenth century boasted a police force and a judiciary that imprisoned or executed "liberals" (see Giuseppe Verdi's *Tosca*). It was also the last conclave to be held in the Quirinal, the pope's Roman summer residence until the collapse of the Papal States in 1870. (Since then it has been the official residence of the president of Italy.)

It proved a bruising contest. The leading candidates were Cardinal L. Lambruschini, who wanted to continue the highly conservative policies of Gregory XVI, who notoriously banned railroads on the grounds that *chemins de fer* (railways) were *chemins d'enfer* (ways to hell). His chief opponent, Giovanni Maria Mastai, bishop of Imola, blithely brought along the latest pamphlets depicting papal primacy as the hope of liberal Italy. His intention was to present them to the new pope.

On June 14, 1846, those cardinals capable of walking processed from the church of San Silvestro (now the titular church of Cardinal Basil Hume) to the Quirinal. Mastai may not have expected to become pope, but behind the scenes two important cardinals were working in his behalf. The Roman cardinal Polidori joined forces with Cardinal Micara to organize the defeat of Lambruschini. This introduces the concept of the *grande elettore*, the pope makers who intrigue on behalf of others but are not themselves candidates.

The 1846 election also dramatized the issue of continuity or change that, with many variants, is always at issue in a conclave. Mastai's supporters wanted a different sort of papacy, one that would take the lead in uniting Italy and "modernizing" the Papal States; Lambruschini, as the dauphin of Gregory XVI, wanted to continue his counterrevolutionary policies.

In the first ballot of June 15, Lambruschini had 15 votes to Mastai's 13; by the second ballot Mastai was ahead 17–13. The next day Mastai led 27–11 in the third ballot and clinched it with 36–10 in the fourth. However, this victory in the fourth ballot was secured by a now-banned device called *accessus:* when the result of a ballot was announced, and before proceeding to the next vote, a cardinal could announce that he was annulling his previous vote and rallying to the majority. The cardinal scrutineers *(recognitores)* made the switch. On this occasion in 1846 nine cardinals did so. The maneuver, of course, meant that for those who changed their minds *the ballot was not secret;* so they could be—and were—accused of currying favor or seeking influence with the pope they helped to elect. That is why this custom was abolished.

Pius IX was the last pope of the *ancien régime* in every sense of the term. He ruled over a court in which the favor and patronage of the prince were all-decisive for the careers of his courtiers. His short-lived "liberalism" was largely confined to matters such as railways and gas lighting. "We had reckoned on everything," said Metternich, "except a liberal pope." He did not have long to worry about that.

MORAL: The cardinals do not always get what they bargain for. They elect a man on one set of assumptions, only to find he does something completely different. Soon the liberal pope was fleeing revolution in Rome to Gaeta in 1849, disguised as a woman.

That same year the Polish romantic poet Juliusz Slowacki, exiled in Paris, wrote a poem in which he forecast that the twentieth century would see a Slavic pope:

This pope will not—Italian-like—take fright
At cannon's roar or sabre-thrust
but brave as God himself stand and give fight—
His world—but dust. . .
Love he dispenses as great powers today
Distribute arms:
With sacramental power—his sole array—
The world he charms.

As a boy in Katowice and Kraków, Karol Wojtyla, the future Pope John Paul II, knew Slowacki's poem by heart.

Pius was coldly received by the Roman populace in 1846 when he showed himself to them on June 17—partly because rumor based on the size of habits ordered by the papal tailor suggested a more popular and different-shaped candidate, Cardinal Gizzi. So sure were Gizzi's servants that his election was in the bag that they had already rashly burned his cardinal's robes.

If rumor has largely ceased to be a factor in papal elections, the first appearance of a new pope before the Roman people remains an important test: it is a last faint flicker of the participation of the people of Rome in the election of their bishop. His "reception" by the Roman People of God still counts.

Both John Paul I and John Paul II were warmly received by the Roman people. Albino Luciani, patriarch of Venice, won them by his charm and choice of double-barreled name. Having neither the wisdom of heart of Pope

John XXIII nor the vast experience of Paul VI, he appealed to both of them. On his death, posters went up anticipating and welcoming "Pope John Paul II." Cardinal Karol Wojtyla accepted this name, though he would have preferred Stanislaus. He won the Romans with his lilting Italian and by the fact that he was Polish.

When Leo XIII was elected in 1878, he was not able to "show himself" to the Roman populace. With the collapse of the Papal States in 1870, the pope had become the self-styled "prisoner of the Vatican." Thus immured, he was unable to go about his diocese of Rome and left it in the charge of his vicar. Pius IX had been extremely unpopular, especially in anticlerical circles. Cries of "Throw the old dolt into the river" were heard as his body was being transferred to its final resting place.

The election of Gioacchino Pecci as Leo XIII came as a relief after the thirty-two years of Pio Nono, but it was not a surprise. Bonghi's book had prepared minds for Leo's election.

MORAL: Cardinals, even when created by the pope just deceased and on the whole admiring him, do not necessarily vote for someone in the same mold.

Whereas Pius IX had rejected modernity, Leo XIII sought prudently to embrace it. Although restricted in what he could do in Italy—he remained the "prisoner of the Vatican"—he patched up the quarrel with Germany after the disastrous Kulturkampf, sought the friendship of England, made peace with Switzerland, did his best to rally nostalgic French Catholics to their republic, tried to be on good terms with the czar of Russia, and even wrote to the emperor of China inviting him to protect missionaries.

One of Leo's first acts was to make John Henry Newman, the most celebrated convert of the nineteenth century, a cardinal. He revived the study of the philosophy and theology of Saint Thomas Aquinas *(Aeterni Patris)*. He opened the Vatican Library to scholars, declaring that "the Church has nothing to fear from the truth." Most important of all, with *Rerum Novarum* in 1891, he inaugurated the Church's "social teaching" denouncing impartially unbridled collectivism and unbridled individualism (or liberalism). This set the pattern for subsequent pontiffs. The anniversary of *Rerum Novarum* was marked by *Quadragesimo Anno* in 1931, *Octogesimo Anno* in 1971, and by John Paul II's *Centesimus Annus* in 1991. Never before had an encyclical letter been so influential and positive. It showed that the loss of the Papal States had liberated the papacy for a more spiritual role on the international scene.

Leo XIII was sixty-seven when elected in 1888. Conventional conclave wisdom said (and still says) that is about the right age, leading to an active pontificate of about ten years. But Leo XIII went on and on, celebrating his twenty-fifth anniversary as pope in 1903 when he was an astonishing ninety-three. As often happens, the cardinal electors of 1888 may have got what they bargained for, but they also got more than they had bargained for.

This made the conclave of 1903, at the dawn of the twentieth century, particularly fraught with tension. With sixty-three cardinal electors, the successful candidate had to reach two-thirds, or forty-two. The candidate most suited to continue the open-minded policies of Leo XIII was Mariano Rampolla, his secretary of state, the man effectively in charge as Leo aged. Rampolla was in the lead for the first two days, gaining twenty-four votes in the first ballot, twenty-nine in the second and third, and reaching thirty in the fourth. Then he stalled. His main opponent, Cardinal Gotti, had a mere seventeen.

The usual explanation for Rampolla's failure is that the cardinal archbishop of Kraków, Kniaz de Kolzielsko Puzyna, exercised the "veto" on behalf of the Austrian emperor, Franz-Joseph. That would mean that the conclave secret had been breached. Certainly this was the twentieth-century conclave most conditioned by political considerations on the part of the leading "Catholic" power of the day (republican and anticlerical France having forfeited this role). But it was not the only factor. An intransigent opposition of five cardinals was determined to stop Rampolla. In the first ballot they voted for Giuseppe Sarto, patriarch of Venice. Their votes and those that had gone to Gotti made up the one-third needed to block Rampolla. Manifestly he could not win, and his votes declined from the fifth ballot to twenty-four, then to thirteen and ten. Sarto played the card of humility: after the fourth ballot he declared, "I will renounce the cardinalate and become a Capuchin friar."[6] It seemed to work, for he had thirty-five votes in the sixth ballot, and in the seventh he became pope.

MORAL: Mistrust false humility and simple-minded piety masquerading as pastoral policy.

Sarto made his intentions clear by taking the name Pius. The pontificate of Leo XIII had been an interlude between the two Piuses. At first the comparison with his predecessor worked to his advantage. Pius X was simpler and more homely. Though Leo had received Catholics—with the exception of cardinals, kings, and princes—on their knees, Pius sat them all down and chatted amiably. No one could have imagined the regally imperious Leo teaching catechism to children or swapping jokes with his coachman. Pius X gave the impression of being an unworldly, unpolitical, spiritual pope, the whole world's parish priest.

It was a faulty impression. Pius X, a simple-minded man, was obsessed with orthodoxy. This comes through even in the historical study (known as *Disquisitio*) designed to promote his beatification. He saw perils everywhere. His 1907 encyclical, *Pascendi*, first invented "Modernism" as a pernicious theological system and then condemned it with great vigor. It included a disciplinary section, which meant commissions of enquiry in all dioceses of Italy (at least) and wholesale oustings of seminary professors. Pius X encouraged purges, witch-hunts, and denunciations. The efficient espionage system, organized by Monsignor Umberto Benigni, was exposed thanks to the accidental discovery of a cache of documents in Ghent during World War I. The *Disquisitio* pretends that Pius X had nothing directly to do with these events and blames overzealous subordinates.

Pius X died on August 20, 1914, his heart broken, said his hagiographers, by the outbreak of a war he had warned against but been unable to prevent. After the shambles of the 1903 conclave, Pius X imposed even stricter secrecy rules. This did not prevent the Austrian foreign minister, Count Berchtold, from instructing his ambassador to the Holy See: "Cardinal Ferrata is considered Francophile and Cardinal Maffi is too much of an Italian nationalist, while the Benedictine Serafini seems the most pious, learned and free from political prejudices." Serafini, in short, would be the least troublesome candidate for the Central Powers.

But the plan or plot did not work. The mood of the conclave was somber, with cardinals from all the belligerents present. The French Jesuit Louis Billot had already lost a nephew on the front. Fifty-seven cardinals went into the conclave, eight being absent for reasons of ill health. The four ballots on September 1 showed Giacomo Della Chiesa, archbishop of Bologna, neck and neck with Maffi but gradually nosing ahead: 12–12, 16–16, 18–16, 21–15.

That evening the cardinal archbishop of Cologne, Hartmann, sensing the danger, remarked that ". . . to elect Della Chiesa would be an affront to the memory of Pius X, since he had been under-secretary of state under Rampolla in the time of Leo XIII, and had continued to work in the spirit of Leo thus causing his removal to Bologna."[7] Della Chiesa was described as "mediocre," no more than a good bureaucrat, and characterized by a "violent temper."

The slanderous discrediting of candidates has been a feature of conclaves. It is rarely effective, and sometimes boomerangs. In 1914 it failed altogether. The majority of Cardinals thought being different from Pius X and reviving the spirit of Leo XIII a positive advantage as Europe plunged headlong into the most devastating war it had hitherto known. With Maffi dropped, the Benedictine Serafini became leader of the opposition. On September 2, Della Chiesa gradually consolidated his lead: 20–10, 27–17, 31–21, and 32–21. But he still needed six more votes, which he just barely achieved on September 3, winning 38–18.

Of the three American cardinals, only Cardinal John J. Farley, archbishop of New York, described as "liberal for an American," actually managed to vote. He had prudently positioned himself in Switzerland. At this time cardinals had ten days to get to Rome. William H. O'Connell of Boston and the eighty-year-old James Gibbons of Baltimore did their best to beat the deadline, with O'Connell hiring a limousine in Naples. But it made no difference. They arrived together in Rome to the sound of bells and rejoicing at the election of Della Chiesa.[8]

MORAL: Cardinals should never say, or think, that they cannot elect *X* or *Y* because to do so would constitute "an insult to the memory of his predecessor still warm in his grave."

The new pope made his intentions clear in his choice of name: Benedict XV. Benedict had been the name of the fictional pope in Antonio Fogazzaro's novel *Il Santo*, which Pius X had ludicrously put on the Index of Forbidden Books. As far as possible, he would be a pope of peace, which led him in 1917 to declare the war "a useless slaughter" *(inutile strage)*, a phrase that united all the belligerents against him. It was repeated by Pope John Paul II during the Gulf War of 1991.

But the clearest sign of Benedict's repudiation of the policies of his predecessor came in his first encyclical letter, *Ad Beatissimi* of November 1, 1914. It put an end to the habit of witch-hunting and denunciations, which appeared blasphemously irrelevant as Europe plunged into a fratricidal civil war. "There is no need to add epithets to the profession of Catholicism," said Benedict, "it is enough for each to say, *"Christianus mihi nomen, Catholicus cognomen* [Christian is my name, and Catholic is my family name]. What matters is to live up to these names in one's life."

Because candidates for the papacy are not allowed to present an electoral platform, their first encyclical is often a programmatic statement, a declaration of intent. Benedict's misfortune was to be elected pope at a time when Europe was deafened by heavy artillery fire. He deserves rehabilitation. He emptied the Vatican coffers to provide humanitarian aid to Soviet Russia. He enabled Italian Catholics to return to political life by agreeing to the foundation of the *Partito Popolare Italiano.* Under its first secretary (that is, leader), the fiery and profound Sicilian priest Don Luigi Sturzo, it was the main challenger to the rise of Fascism. He reorganized Catholic missions, shifting their headquarters from Paris to Rome. He was urged to write an encyclical on nationalism as the greatest scourge and heresy of the twentieth century. Though willing enough, he ran out of time, dying within five days of flu that unexpectedly turned into pneumonia. He was "only" sixty-seven. There was much that his successor could build upon.

Benedict died on January 17, 1922. Giovanni Battista Montini, then twenty-five, snuffling with his annual bout of flu, sketched out a portrait of "the sort of pope" the Church needed:

> *The Church is about to be embodied in a man who after twenty centuries should represent not only the powerful Christ but the Christ who is evangelical, peace-loving, holy and poor. Let us pray that we may merit a pope who is very like Jesus; and for that he will have to be crucified by the world that hates what is not its own; its salvation demands as much.*[9]

It would be forcing matters to call this prophetic. The young Montini was looking forward to the election in 1958 of John XXIII, whom he would meet two years later, in 1925.

His evangelical and "utopian" vision of the papacy was hardly fulfilled by Achille Ratti, who emerged on February 6, 1922, after the bloodiest conclave of the twentieth century.

Two cardinals, at least, were excommunicated for breaking the rules. According to the *Memoirs* of Cardinal Pietro Gasparri, which languish unpublished in the Vatican Archives, they were La Fontaine, patriarch of Venice, and the Anglophile Rafael Merry del Val, both of whom were associated with the repressive policies of Saint Pius X. A Roman "joke" (that is, a witticism with a point) said that Merry del Val, son of the Spanish ambassador to London, could never be beatified, for then there would be no one to blame for Pius X's mistakes.

Now patriarch of Venice, La Fontaine had been prefect of the Consistorial Congregation and therefore Grand Inquisitor supreme under Pius X. Among his victims or near-misses was the young Angelo Roncalli, the future Pope John XXIII. Merry del Val, educated in England during his father's term as ambassador, had been Saint Pius's secretary of state at the age of thirty-five. To call them conservatives would be an understatement. But the reason they were excommunicated was that they tried to do a deal with Achille Ratti, who, after a hesitant start, soon became the favorite. He could have their votes, they intimated, provided he did not have Pietro Gasparri as secretary of state.

Gasparri, principal author of the code of canon law, which improbably appeared in 1917, had been Benedict XV's secretary of state. Continuity suggested he would be an obvious choice for the succession. But the supporters of Pius X, still miffed by the "mistake" of 1914, were resolved to block Gasparri. In this conclave, much of the hard work happened during the *Novemdiales*, the nine days of mourning that precede the locking up in the Apostolic Palace. Secrecy at this point is not always watertight.

Even though the Austro-Hungarian Empire had ceased to exist, fragmented into a multiplicity of small states, Austria still aspired to play a role in the conclave. Vienna, by now a very large head on a very small body, shrewdly appointed the Baron Ludwig von Pastor as its ambassador. Since Leopold von Ranke in the nineteenth century, nobody knew more about the papacy than von Pastor. His *History of the Popes* remains indispensable. There was still, he held, a role for Austria in a conclave. It was the last time anyone could cherish this illusion.

On January 27, 1922, von Pastor met Cardinal Piffl off the train from Vienna. The German-speaking cardinals met for a noncommittal *tour d'horizon*. Piffl's diary records the result of their eve-of-conclave discussions: "Five qualities seem to be required of the new pope. 1) A deep religious life. 2) a diplomat. 3) a learned man. 4) a man well versed in politics. 5) a correct attitude towards the Italian government."[10] That seemed to mean someone who was prepared to work for reconciliation with Italy and so to solve the "Roman Question"—that is, what to do about the lost Papal States.

As often happens, it was easier to sketch out a job description for the papacy than to find a candidate to realize it. The Dutch cardinal William Van Rossum, longtime resident in Rome, prefect of the Congregation of Propaganda (that is, missions), otherwise known as the "red pope," was the main *grande elettore*.

In his view, the time had come for a non-Italian pope. He was thinking not of himself but of Merry del Val. Though somewhat premature, the idea was not totally absurd. Its weakness was that, after a lifetime in Rome, non-Italian cardinals lost their national identity and became "more Italian than the Italians." This was certainly true of Merry del Val; he appeared as little more than a clone of Pius X, who had promoted him from nothing. Once again the two American cardinals, William H. O'Connell of Boston and Dennis Dougherty, archbishop of Philadelphia, were mortified to arrive at Rome's Termini station half an hour after the pope had been elected.[11]

MORAL: Do not see cardinals as idealistic dreamers, ignorant of the mechanisms of power.

Ratti took the name Pius XI and personified the Church of his period: tough-minded, unyielding, and vigorous in the defense of the institutional rights of the Church in the age of dictators.

The conclave of March 1939 was the briefest and most predictable of the century so far. After the Munich crisis of the previous autumn, war was inevitable. The usual debate about a "spiritual" or a "diplomatic" pope was settled in favor of the most experienced and brilliant diplomat available, Roman-born Eugenio Pacelli, his predecesor's secretary of state since 1929. He had been nuncio in Bavaria and Berlin, where he learned German and read Goethe to perfect his style. He traveled widely—and by airplane—and lunched with President Franklin D. Roosevelt. On this slender basis he was widely considered a "modern" man.

However, Pacelli's election was not a foregone conclusion. The Italian cardinals thought his temperament suspect—a bag of nervous hesitations. His colleague in the Secretariat of State Domenico Tardini put this nicely: "He was by temperament gentle and rather shy. He wasn't a fighter. . . . His great goodness led him to wish to please everyone, and to prefer the path of gentleness to that of severity, to persuade rather than to impose. That explains, if anything does, his silences."[12] It also explains why fourteen cardinals of the Roman Curia obstinately refused to vote for him, even though he had it in the bag. They knew him better than foreigners dazzled by his diplomatic brilliance.

Pius XII was, in short, not a pope for wartime, when, as the British minister said, one needed not a *Pastor Angelicus* (angelic pastor)—the Malachy-prompted name—but a *Leo Furibundus* (a raging lion). The see of New York was vacant. One of the first and most fateful acts of Pius XII was to appoint Francis J. Spellman archbishop of New York.[13]

MORAL: Be careful of popes who say, "I don't want collaborators but executants."

As Pius XII, Pacelli had a long and increasingly authoritarian reign. Despite popular legend, he was not theologically well educated. If anything, he was a canon lawyer. He tried to remedy his deficiencies by staying up late at night, studying up on, say, the gas industry from encyclopedias in preparation for his next morning's address.

In theology he was a *terrible simplificateur.* Whatever appeared to depart from "the deposit of faith" was anathema. He beatified and canonized Pius X. It was enough for the French Dominican Réginald Garrigou-Lagrange to tell him that the deposit of faith was being gnawed away by French Jesuits and Dominicans for him to act. *Humani Generis* condemned them in 1950. It was the last theological witchhunt of the century—so far. Garrigou-Lagrange, meanwhile, was supervising the thesis "Faith in Saint John of the Cross," written by the brilliant twenty-seven-year-old Polish priest Karol Wojtyla.

Pius XII nearly died in 1954. Cardinals packed their bags; diplomats prepared their memos; journalists speculated. The Italian ambassador to the Holy See, Dr. Mameli, wrote a revealing report that admirably sums up what "informed sources" were saying at the time.

Mameli says that to penetrate the thickets of the next conclave, three questions have to be faced:

> Papa italiano o Papa straniero? *An Italian or a foreigner?*
> Papa politico o Papa religioso? *A political or a religious Pope?*
> starà nella media dell'età o no? *A middle-aged Pope or not?*[14]

Mameli did not expect the election of a "young pope." The composition of the college of cardinals suggested that they would not buy any such idea. "An older pope would be more acceptable to them, especially if the idea of a *transitional pontificate* came to be accepted."

The Italian ambassador, having unknowingly provided the principle that would govern the conclave that actually did take place in 1958, then mooted names. He left aside Giuseppe Siri (why? too young? too close to Pius XII?) and offered a classic list of three "safe" men (Alfredo Ottaviani, Giacomo Lercaro, Ernesto Ruffini). But he added that "outsiders" (in English) like Mimmi could come through. His most "prophetic" remark came in an aside: "If the idea of a 'diplomatic' pope prevails, then there are various nuncios created in the last consistory [of 1953] who are between seventy and seventy-three. In some circles the name of Roncalli, Patriarch of Venice, is mentioned, as bringing together the two qualities of 'diplomat' and 'religious.'" Add his "transitional" quality—the fact that he would not be around for very long—and his election seems almost inevitable.

Mameli hit another nail on the head when he suggested that Roncalli's rival could well be Agagianian, the Armenian prefect of propaganda. But he was only a "token" foreigner, having been thoroughly romanized. "We two went up and down like two chick peas in a pot," said Pope John afterward.[15]

Angelo Roncalli, who would emerge from the 1958 conclave as pope, was concerned about Pius XII's illness in 1954 but even more worried by Gaston Bardet, a French would-be prophet who had sent him a proof copy of his latest book. Roncalli, now patriarch of Venice, replied that this "mis-mash of predictions bears all the marks of the 'spirit of confusion'"—in other words, it came from the devil. In January 1955 Roncalli wrote to his sister, Maria: "Some mad Frenchman, who has revelations and second sight, has even given the name I will take when they make me pope. Mad, mad the whole lot of them. I'm thinking rather of death. I have a full programme of work for this year and also for next year."[16] All well and good: but *what name* did the Frenchman say he would take? I am morally sure he predicted John. *Vocabor Johannes* (I will be called John) was not a surprise for him as it was for everyone else.

In 1958, however, was the first conclave at which an American cardinal was considered seriously *papabile*. Francis J. Spellman thought he still had a chance. This was an illusion, as his biographer explains: "Another strike against Spellman was his nationality. An American pope would give credence to Communist claims that the Vatican was the tool of the United States."[17] He was also regarded as too "political" and "unspiritual." In the end, the "American era" resulted in the building of the North American College and the Villa Stritch as the residence for Americans working in the Curia.

MORAL: The bookies get it wrong, and the Holy Spirit has his little jokes—the transitional pope became the pope of the Church's transition.

Having devoted the whole of chapter 20 to the 1963 conclave in *Paul VI: The First Modern Pope*, I can be brief on it here. Giovanni Battista Montini, archbishop of Milan, was expected to win, and did. The contest was fierce. His principal rival was Cardinal Giacomo Lercaro, archbishop of Bologna, who had undergone a startling conversion in the pontificate of Pope John. The bookmakers' odds fluctuated wildly. Bernard Pawley, the first permanent Anglican representative in Rome, reported to the archbishops of Canterbury and York:

> *Montini is played down while Lercaro is played up in his place. In public opinion Confalonieri the favorite. Urbani of Venice and Costaldo of Naples increasingly canvassed. So put them on a "long list". . . . In the present state of tension, nobody will get the candidate they really want, and they will have to agree on a "third man."*[18]

He was learning the lingo, if not the ropes, fast. Every speculator needs a "long list" and a "short list"; and he needs a "third man" as a "compromise candidate" to break the deadlock. But these considerations apart, Pawley's presence and remarks show how important papal conclaves have become for all Christians.

The fact that a "third man" was not needed in 1963 does not mean that it was not close run. At one point Cardinal Gustavo Testa, a fat friend of Pope John from Bergamo, lost his temper and told his neighbor, in a stage whisper loud enough to be heard all round the Sistine Chapel, that "they should stop their squalid maneuverings and consider the good of the Church." This broke the rules. Voting should be done in silence. But Testa was right. When it was all over, he said, "Hair-raising things happened in this conclave—I will have to ask the pope's permission to speak about them." He never did.

Anyway, Montini scraped home on the sixth ballot, gaining only two more votes than the required fifty-seven. As Cardinal Lercaro knelt before him, Paul VI said to him, "So that is the way life goes, your eminence, you should really be sitting here now."

MORAL: In this case, the moral was drawn by the new pope himself: after the "hair-raising things"—attempts to strike deals and determine the future course of the council—Paul VI determined to reform the rules of the conclave. How he did that, and what its effects were, are the subjects of the next chapter.

Pope John Paul II in 1993 at Mile High Stadium in
Denver, Colorado, during World Youth Day celebrations.

ABOVE: Cardinals gathered in the Sistine Chapel, October 14, 1978, before the conclave that elected Pope John Paul II.

RIGHT: Ballots were burned in this small stove at the conclave that elected Pope John XXIII in 1958.

TOP: Cardinal Francis Arinze, Cardinal Roger Etchegaray
BOTTOM: Cardinal Bernardin Gantin, Cardinal Basil Hume

TOP: Cardinal Pio Laghi, Cardinal Jean-Marie Lustiger
BOTTOM: Cardinal Roger M. Mahony

TOP: Cardinal Carlo Maria Martini, Cardinal Lucas Moreira Neves
BOTTOM: Cardinal Joseph Ratzinger

TOP: Cardinal Nicholas Lopez Rodriguez, Cardinal Achille Silvestrini
BOTTOM: Cardinal Alfonso Lopez Trujillo

THREE How Paul VI's Reforms Worked

Paul VI would have been a *reforming* pope even if Vatican II had never happened. What he chiefly wanted to reform was the Roman Curia, the bureaucracy by which the pope administers the Church. In 1942, in the darkest days of the war, he told Galeazzo Ciano, Mussolini's son-in-law and foreign minister, that the Roman Curia would have to lose its "Italian" character and be properly internationalized.

One way to do this would have been to have more Americans in high curial places. After the death of Cardinal Luigi Maglione in August 1944, Pius XII desperately wanted Cardinal Francis J. Spellman, archbishop of New York, to succeed him as secretary of state. Spellman's diary recalls how, with tears in his eyes, Pius XII confided this intention to him in September 1944. But it would have to wait. For with the war not yet over, it would never do for a cardinal from one of the belligerents to become secretary of state. In the meantime, "Vessels," the espionage service that was the ancestor of the CIA, discovered this scheme and made it known, thus ruining it. Heartbroken at the failure of his plan, which would in his mind have signaled a new "American era" in the Church, Pius XII determined not to appoint a secretary of state at all.

The man left in charge was Montini. He knew that to reform the Curia was to reform the papacy. In 1950 he mused aloud with Riccardo Lombardi, S.J., on the need for a much simplified and more evangelical papacy. He outlined his vision:

> *Let the Pope leave the Vatican with all those in it, let him leave them with their stipends and go off, at least for certain periods, to St. John Lateran; there he would live with his seminarians, with his people, with a new ritual. . . . He could return to the Vatican from time to time. And in St. John Lateran he would begin a new way of governing the Church, like Peter who was a poor man.*[1]

It is facile to point that out, as Pope Montini did not follow his own advice. Any pope works within certain constraints.

Yet he did his best to reform the Curia inherited from Pius XII and largely left intact by John XXIII. The crucial point was to impose a retirement age on cardinals. Without it, cardinals behaved like medieval barons able to go on empire building until they died. Paul VI changed all that with *Regimini Ecclesiae* of 1967. Moreover, he struck another blow against gerontocracy by insisting that all offices should last for not more than five years, be renewable only once, and be relinquished on the accession of a new pope.

Paul's reforming streak was enormously strengthened by Vatican II. Every role and task in the Church was held up for inspection and marked for renewal: priest, layperson, religious, bishop, missionary. But there was one exception: the papal office itself did not come under scrutiny, nor did the college of cardinals. The best, and probably the only, way in which he could reform the papacy was by the manner he exercised it. Pope John modified the practice of the papacy whatever the theory, refusing, for example, the notion of producing "infallible" statements. Paul did the same, though in more unobtrusive ways, making himself a leader in ecumenical affairs and his office a possible rallying point for the unity of all Christians.

The college of cardinals was a fit subject for reform. Medieval creations with no scriptural foundation, cardinals stuck out like sore thumbs in the era of collegiality. Where was the Church? Vatican II taught that the Church existed in and through local congregations: the church in Harlem or the church in Westminster. This was a return to New Testament usage, where *church* was as often plural as singular: the churches of Ephesus and Corinth, and the seven churches of Asia mentioned in the Apocalypse, made up the one church that was the Body of Christ. That was an important Vatican II rediscovery.

It implied that the bishops, as heads of the local churches, were inserted into the universal Church through their communion with the Bishop of Rome, who inherited from Peter the primacy. So the pope presides over the whole assembly of charity. It is not just a matter of adding up the local churches. All the bishops of the world form a college or team with their president. This the council called "collegiality."

In this scheme the key, indeed, essential, players were bishops and archbishops; but cardinals did not fit in. A common theological opinion summed up by René Laurentin held that "it was an anomaly, if not a scandal, that the episcopal college existing by divine right has so very little part in the government of the Church, while the college of cardinals enjoys all the power, privileges, precedence and tenure."[2]

Bishop Christopher Butler, former abbot of Downside, went further still. The logic of Vatican II suggested that, on the death of a pope, authority in the Church devolved upon the college of bishops. So if the college of cardinals enjoyed the privilege of being the sole electors of the pope, they did so only by virtue of some kind of delegation from the world's bishops.[3] Cardinal Léon-Joseph Suenens drew the conclusion: it would be more appropriate for the conclave to be made up of presidents of episcopal conferences, because they formed the truly collegial group representing the whole Church.

Paul VI was sensitive to these arguments, while being awed and perhaps alarmed at the prospect of departing from a precedent nearly a thousand years old. Rather than respond directly, he took a preliminary step. On November 23, 1970, he launched his first missile at the college of cardinals. It took the form of the decree *Ingravescentem Aetatem.* It declared that cardinals over eighty could not take part in a conclave. This move effectively pensioned them off.

As Paul VI, now aged seventy-three, set off for his last papal journey to the Philippines and Australia, ousted cardinals like Alfredo Ottaviani, eighty, and Eugène Tisserant, eighty-six, went on Italian television and waxed formidably indignant. Ottaviani, the baker's son from Trastevere, by now almost totally blind, for so many years the chief watchdog of orthodoxy at the Holy Office, quivered his mighty jowls at the indignity of it all. The papal decision, he spluttered, was "absolutely unheard of, arbitrary, revolutionary, in contempt of a centuries-old tradition." Tisserant, a French cavalry officer in the First World War, conducted his last campaign with panache. He complained that the pope was practicing "moral euthanasia." Both Tisserant and Ottaviani asked what would happen when the Holy Father himself reached eighty. If the over-eighties were deemed incapable of electing a pope, someone over eighty could surely not be considered capable of exercising the office itself.

They had a point. An eighty-year-old pope would have to resign. At this date, it may be surmised, Paul VI did not expect to live to eighty. Tisserant, solid as a rock, said he would outlive Paul VI and looked forward to reaching one hundred in 1985. (In fact, he died some fifteen months later, on February 21, 1972.)

Excluding the over-eighties was an important precedent. It meant that the composition of the conclave was not intangible: it was not set in stone. In such matters, small changes can be as significant as big ones. Ottaviani was right to say that this was a revolutionary decision.

But could Paul VI go further and embrace the Suenens proposal of making the Extraordinary Synod the electoral body? Such an assembly was held in 1969 to deal with the problems that arose after Paul VI rejected artificial birth control in *Humanae Vitae*. It was made up of presidents of episcopal conferences. Some of them happened to be cardinals, but not all were. Could this—should this—be the body to make up the conclave? Some such project was certainly "being studied."

However, on March 5, 1973, addressing the latest batch of cardinals, Paul produced a watered-down version of this plan. The college of cardinals would remain the electoral body, but there would be added to it the fifteen members of the Synod Council (a body set up by the 1971 synod), twelve of whom were elected by their peers (three per continent). A few noncardinals would thus be involved. It would also be good to include Oriental patriarchs.[4]

This proposal created an even greater furor among the Italian cardinals than the exclusion of the over-eighties. Cardinal Giuseppe Siri, of Genoa, a possible pope in all the conclaves of the second half of the century, argued against it in an audience with Paul VI lasting an hour and a half:

> *It was like a game of ping-pong; he listened to my arguments and countered with his own dialectic. I held back till the end one last objection: it was a mistake to put on the same level cardinals who are named by the pope and bishops who are appointed in a different way.*

> *Cardinals are answerable to no one, while bishops have to account for their decisions. So they can be easily "conditioned." This term alarmed Paul VI. "Very well," he said," it will be the sacred college and it alone that will elect the pope." Then I took his hand, kissed his ring, and fled. If I had gone on any more, he would have flung an ash-tray at my head.*[5]

Was Siri the smoker? A large pinch of salt should be applied to this story. Siri typically overestimated his own influence. The idea that cardinals are more genuinely independent than bishops is true only if the bishops desperately want to become cardinals and are thus paralyzed by caution.

Yet after wavering on this question, Paul VI's new legislation, contained in the apostolic constitution *Romano Pontifici Eligendo*, officially dated October 1, 1975, confined the election to cardinals under eighty. It innovated only in its rigor about secrecy, its mania for security inspections, and the terrifying oaths it imposed. Above all, it insisted that cardinals should normally go into the conclave alone, unless they needed serious medical assistance, in which case they had to prove it (art. 45). In the previous more relaxed tradition, approved by Pope John, cardinals were allowed to take in a couple of friends as *conclavistas* and a third if they were ill.

In 1958 Cardinal Francis J. Spellman took in two junior aides. One of them, George A. Schlichte, has left an account of what happened:

> *Spellman sat on the housing committee. We occupied half of a completely furnished apartment with two baths. The ecclesiastical occupant had gotten bumped because he happened to*

*reside within the conclave area. Cardinal Pizzardo and his
one lay assistant occupied one room each, as did Spellman
and his secretary. I slept in a cot in the dining room and
stocked up the refrigerator with extras on the morning of the
lock-up. I saw cardinals with quarters made by curtains at
the ends of corridors and under stairways. All the cardinals
ate meals at one oval table. The rest of us ate at long tables in
a nearby room. After the second morning Spellman announced that he could take these cardinals at lunch and supper but not for breakfast. I then boiled the eggs.*[6]

Paul put a stop to this cheerful informality. The cardinals
would be on their own before God. While in conclave they
were on retreat.

Only the minimum of necessary officials were allowed
in: the papal master of ceremonies, the sacristan (43), some
religious priests for confessions, two doctors with one or
two aides, the architect of the conclave with two technicians (55 and 61). All these are chosen by the majority of
the cardinals on the proposal of the *camerlengo* and his three
cardinal assistants. There will also be an appropriate number of other persons to take care of the material needs of
the conclave; these will be named by the relevant commission of cardinals as mentioned above (13c) (44).

With hangers-on eliminated, those allowed in have to
take an oath that begins:

*I, N.N., promise and swear that I will observe inviolable se-
crecy about each and every matter concerning the election of
the new pontiff which has been discussed or decided in the con-*

gregations of the cardinals, also about whatever happens in the conclave or place of election, directly or indirectly, and finally about the voting and every other matter that may in any way come to my knowledge. . . . (47)

Clearly, the idea was to make the next conclave as water-tight as possible.

But this intention was frustrated by another important clause. The over-eighties were excluded from the conclave: there was no going back on that. But they were not excluded, indeed they were invited, to the discussions that preceded the entry into the conclave, known as "general congregations." Paul VI prescribed (art. 37) that at least fifteen and not more than twenty days should elapse between the death of a pope and the entry into the conclave. Cardinals would join in the general congregations just as soon as they arrived at Rome's Leonardo da Vinci airport. Many of them, preoccupied with their pastoral work, would not feel a great sense of urgency. They would not make haste.

Those cardinals already in place in Rome would have an advantage in these early stages. Even if they did not have undue influence—which cannot be excluded—they would watch with great keenness an event from which they felt most unjustly excluded. Cardinal Carlo Confalonieri, a *conclavista* in 1922 when Pius XI was elected, observed the "smokes" of 1978 from his rooftop garden. Not to tell him, in the strictest confidence, of course, how the voting went would be cruel indeed. But because he was not in the conclave, he was not under oath.

So in the end *Romano Pontifici Eligendo*, which has not been revised and therefore is still in force, will be the guide to the next conclave as it was to the two conclaves of 1978. John Paul II, who has not hesitated to innovate when he felt like it, has not touched the conclave. Perhaps he thinks that to do so would be to invalidate the process by which he was elected.

Anyway, *Romano Pontifici Eligendo* describes the procedure that was adopted in 1978. Because the same rules will apply next time, a brief outline can serve as a guide to what happens. There is no voting on the opening evening. However, the cardinals have to sit through a reading of extracts from Paul VI's document, particularly numbers 55–61 concerning secrecy. Anyone unwise enough to introduce "technical instruments, of whatever kind, for the recording, reproduction, transmission of voices and images" (61) into the conclave would be immediately expelled.

Next comes the solemn oath by which the cardinals swear to follow the apostolic constitution, to defend the rights of the Holy See, to refuse all secular vetoes on the election, and to keep the whole thing secret.

In view of what happened in 1978, the precise wording of the secrecy oath is worth giving:

Above all, we promise and swear to observe with the greatest fidelity and with all persons, including the conclavists, the secret concerning what takes place in the conclave or place of election, directly or indirectly, concerning the scrutinies; not to break this secret in any way, either during the conclave or after the election of the new Pontiff, unless we are given explicit au-thorization from the same Pontiff (49).

This was sworn on the Gospels with each cardinal adding, "So help me God and these Holy Gospels that I touch with my hand."

After the oath, the cardinals were allowed to go to bed in rooms that are quaintly called "cells." The oldest and most fragile were lodged next to the Sistine Chapel and the Sala Borgia, where meals were taken; the others were assigned rooms by lot the previous day. There were great differences between the cells. Not much had changed since 1958. Some were poky little offices, tucked away in odd corners, with discolored patches on the walls where charts or pictures had been removed. Others were vast Renaissance reception rooms, where the ceilings were forty feet high, and the cardinal, after putting out his chandelier for the night, would have to pick his way nimbly round vast tables and capacious sofas.

But whether in a dingy office or a marble hall, the equipment was modest and standardized: a bed borrowed from the infirmary of Propaganda Fide (the missionary college); a red-shaded lamp too faint to read a breviary by; a washbasin, soap (Donge of Paris), a bucket for slops and a packet of tissues; a writing table with notepaper and an ashtray; a prie-dieu.

All that spartan simplicity was designed to prevent a long conclave, especially in the summer. The impression of living in an "airless tomb"—as Cardinal Siri called it in

1978—could change utterly if the quasi-hotel, discussed at the end of this chapter, is completed in time for the next conclave.

However, in August 1978, the austere monastic seclusion lasted only a day. The conclave was all over by the evening of August 26, and Albino Luciani, patriarch of Venice, emerged as pope and invented the double-barreled name John Paul to honor both his predecessors. The swiftness of the election—there is a scholarly dispute about whether there were three or four ballots—brought out the importance of the preconclave discussions in preparing the conclave.

After the election the eighty-five-year-old Cardinal Carlo Confalonieri was asked on Italian television whether he was surprised:

> *It was certainly not a surprise for me or the other cardinals. The name of Cardinal Luciani was one that had attracted the attention of the cardinal electors in the last days of the preconclave period. . . . I have to admit that, at the start, a number of cardinals did not know him well, but this was no longer so after the various daily meetings held under my presidency.*

Quite clearly, he had worked for "his" candidate. So the sixteen over-eighties, mostly Romans like Confalonieri, were without a vote but not without influence. The preconclave meetings had a determining role in fixing what they were looking for and getting to know one another.

The time was spent listening to official reports from the Secretariat of State about the situation of the Church. There was a brief furor at the vagueness of the financial report presented by Cardinal Egidio Vagnozzi, formerly apostolic delegate in Washington. Cardinal Jean Villot, secretary of state and *camerlengo*, ordered him to omit detailed references to shares and property on the grounds that "the African cardinals would not understand these matters and would draw God knows what conclusions."[7] This was politically incorrect. Cardinal Pietro Palazzini demanded to know why the Institute of Religious Works (IOR), commonly known as the Vatican Bank and headed by Archbishop Paul C. Marcinkus, native of Cicero, Illinois, had not been mentioned. Vagnozzi batted that back. It was treacherous terrain.

There were 111 cardinals—more than ever before. "How many fresh faces there are," remarked Cardinal Stefan Wyszynski, primate of Poland, to the cardinal archbishop of Kraków, Karol Wojtyla. Wyszynski, at seventy-eight too old to be a candidate, presented a report in which he contrasted the situation in Poland, where the Church had gained more concessions from the Communists than anywhere else, with the pitiable state of churches where bishops had been imposed by the regime. This brought a brisk riposte from the Hungarian cardinal László Lékai, the man who had replaced Cardinal Jozsef Mindszenty, who saw some merit in Marxism.

Wyszynski's report was critical of Paul VI's *Ostpolitik*, which the Polish bishops had never liked. They found it too feeble, compromising, an easy prey for ruthless Communists. They wanted a tougher, more resolute approach. It was easy to pass from being critical of Paul's *Ostpolitik* to being critical of him generally. On the right he was regarded as hesitant and vacillating, making his mind up too late or not at all about contraception, clerical celibacy, religious life, and the other postconciliar problems. The critics of Paul VI were dubbed the "Roman party."

Their candidate was Cardinal Giuseppe Siri, archbishop of Genoa since 1946. Described as "the arch-conservatives' arch-conservative," he thought the pontificate of Pope John XXIII a disaster for the Church (though he later relented before the beatification investigation) and resisted Vatican II changes. Curial cardinals knew that they were out of the reckoning, because after Vatican II the emphasis was on pastoral rather than bureaucratic experience. Siri could claim abundant pastoral experience in Genoa. He would be just the man to take firm grip of the rudder of Peter's barque.

Indeed, he volunteered for the job. In the second of the mourning sermons, Siri reminded the cardinals that the "Holy Spirit" had not abolished their responsibility: "I think I have a duty to warn my fellow cardinals of the task that is before them and which they cannot elude by saying, 'This is what the Holy Spirit thinks.' Nor should they abandon themselves, without toil and suffering, to their first impulse or to unreasonable suggestions." What on earth did he mean? No doubt he had in mind the "pressures" being put on the conclave by theologians and journalists who wanted a pastoral pope, committed to Vatican II, who could also smile. The cardinals should disdain such emotional claptrap and vote for the man of experience, himself.

This suggestion alarmed the majority of the cardinals. They might be critical of some of Paul VI's hesitations, but that did not mean they regarded Vatican II as misguided. But who could carry this standard? Cardinal Sergio Pignedoli, a man of great charm and international friendships, seemed a likely runner. But he was a curialist, he was "too close" to Paul VI (he had been his auxiliary in Milan), and he allegedly had made a famous gaffe in Libya.

The name of Albino Luciani, patriarch of Venice, began to be heard. He would be the candidate of continuity with Paul VI but "continuity with a smile." While the press pool was visiting the conclave area on the eve of the conclave, I met an old friend who shall be called Monsignor Ossobuco. "I cannot tell you who will be pope," he said, "no one can; but ask yourself, Who is Cardinal Benelli's candidate?" Giovanni Benelli had been Paul VI's right-hand man and closest colleague. Though it broke his heart, Paul sent Benelli to Florence in June 1977 as archbishop and made him a cardinal so that he could avoid his own fate in 1954: he had been sent to Milan as archbishop but without a cardinal's hat, thus missing the conclave of 1958.

Now Benelli would be the king-maker rather than the king, the *grande elettore*. From his vantage point as *sostituto* to Paul VI, Benelli knew the college of cardinals better than anyone. He was an implacable opponent of Siri. He had seen Luciani at work among the northern Italian bishops and saw he was friendly, able, with great skills in communication. If an Italian pastoral bishop was wanted, he was the logical candidate.

Chance friendships also helped Luciani. Cardinal Paulo Evaristo Arns, archbishop of Sao Paulo, Brazil, was made a cardinal in 1973 at the same time. Arns says they talked about the Church of the poor and the Third World. Another Brazilian Franciscan, Cardinal Aloisio Lorscheider, archbishop of Fortaleza, invited Luciani to Brazil in 1976 to deal with the pastoral problems of Italian workers. Luciani was better known in Latin America, where his words were reported in the press, than even in Italy. On his return from Brazil in 1976, Luciani told a Venetian priest that he would be happy to see Lorscheider as pope. "He is a man of faith and culture," he said, "and he has a good knowledge of Italy and of Italian." He then added, "The time has come to choose a pope from the Third World."

In that he proved mistaken. But by the time of the conclave Lorscheider's view was that if it was somewhat premature to expect a pope from the Third World, then someone who "loved the Third World" was the next best thing. None of this guaranteed his election, and one cannot speak of collusion in advance.

The proof is that the first ballot on the morning of August 26 revealed a vast scatter of names. The leaders were these:

25	Siri, Giuseppe
23	Luciani, Albino
18	Pignedoli, Sergio
9	Baggio, Sebastiano
8	König, Franz

The Sistine Chapel chimney emitted black or at least grayish smoke. The second ballot followed immediately. Siri lost only one vote, Pignedoli only three, but nearly all the votes for individual candidates drifted to Luciani, who gained thirty. The leaders in the second ballot were these:

53	Luciani
24	Siri
15	Pignedoli
4	Wojtyla

With hindsight, the appearance of Wojtyla is significant. If the top "non-Italian," König, dropped out, then someone was trying to say that the next "non-Italian" in the line was the cardinal archbishop of Kraków. But there was no time to think of that. As they came out of the Sistine Chapel, the Hungarian Lékai remarked to Luciani, "Your votes are increasing." To which the patriarch of Venice, perhaps thinking of the heat in the Apostolic Palace, replied, "It's just a summer shower." It was time for lunch, and time to consult.

For the next ballot was not till 4:30 in the afternoon. There was a meeting in the cell of Cardinal Vincente Enrique y Tarancón, archbishop of Madrid. Present were all the European "progressives"—Suenens, Alfrink of Utrecht, König—but they were joined by others, the Oxford-educated Pakistani Joseph Cordeiro, for instance. "We talked together," said Enrique y Tarancón, "because we weren't quite sure where we were going." But in fact they were now in the clear.

Sources argue about whether there were two more ballots or only one. *Civiltà Cattolica* prudently remarked that
"Pope John Paul was elected, it *seems*, on the third ballot."
Why that cautious "it seems" from this usually so assured
review? The best hypothesis is that Luciani, though he had
more than the seventy-five votes needed on the third ballot,
was hesitant to accept. The following story confirms that. As
Siri went with Villot and Felici to put to him the formal
question, "Do you accept?" Baggio tugged at his sleeve.
"Advise him to take the name Eugene," said Baggio, "because the last Venetian pope was Eugene IV." "This is not
the right moment to be talking about names," Siri replied,
"when we don't even know he will accept."

Suppose that Luciani, knowing perfectly well that the
rebel conservative Archbishop Marcel Lefebvre had declared in advance he would reject any candidate emerging
from a conclave from which the over-eighties were absent,
then called for a "confirming" vote to put to rest any such
juridical doubts. That would explain the confusion about
whether he was elected at the third or the fourth ballot. It
would also explain why the final ballot was "almost by ac-
clamation" (as Vatican Radio remarked). Cardinal Joseph
Höffner of Cologne said: "There was no need to count the
names because the only name read out by the scrutineers
was that of Luciani." Höffner also disclosed that his first
words, on taking his seat before the altar, were, "God will
forgive you for what you have done to me." They needed
forgiveness, for they had, all unwittingly, put him at great
risk of his life. But this knowledge came only with hind-

sight: his anxious temperament and ignorance of the Roman Curia—he spent much time flicking through the pages of the *Annuario Pontificio* discovering who was who—offset the charm of his smile. But, most of all, no attention had been paid to his state of health. It seemed enough that at sixty-seven he was in the right age bracket and probably good for another eight years.

This view was gravely mistaken. John Paul I lasted only thirty-three days (August 26 to September 28). But there is no need to resort to conspiracy theories or murder plots. I accept John Cornwell's verdict: "John Paul almost certainly died of a pulmonary embolus due to a condition of abnormal coagularity of the blood. He required rest and monitored medication. If these had been prescribed he would almost certainly have survived. The warnings of a mortal illness were clear for all to see; the signs were ignored."[8]

Villot, still secretary of state and once again *camerlengo*, devoted some time in the general congregations to the circumstances of Pope John Paul's death. He admitted that the Vatican press office, in saying that John Paul I was discovered by Father John Magee and that he had been reading *The Imitation of Christ*, had given misleading information. But the idea, proposed by Cardinal Confalonieri, that they should produce a collegial statement on the death of John Paul I was rejected: such matters escaped their competence.[9] They could not, in any case, "create facts."

The mood in the October 1978 conclave was very different from that of August. There was an atmosphere of crisis in the air. *L'Osservatore Romano*, the Vatican daily, hinted at the possibility of a third world war. Rockets were raining down on the Christians of Lebanon. The Red Brigades were again a factor to be reckoned with in Italy. This approach—called by Italians the "strategy of tension"—suggested that a strong pope of great doctrinal firmness was called for.

The *Novemdiales* sermons all pointed in the same direction. They produced an edited version in which John Paul I's liberal impulses were screened out and he was presented as a "pope of restoration." According to Confalonieri, he was a "meteor which unexpectedly lights up the heavens, and then disappears." He had stressed "the integrity of doctrine, the perfection of Christian life, and the great discipline of the Church." This, he intimated, was what drew the vast crowds to the Wednesday audiences, not the superficial freshness of his style and his famous smile. According to Cardinal Siri, "John Paul I spoke with great simplicity on the firmness of Catholic doctrine, on ecclesiastical discipline, and on spirituality which is the basis of human existence."

Siri also made the point that John Paul I had "completed his mission." He had done what he had to do. The same note was struck by Cardinal Timothy Manning of Los Angeles: "He made his statement—and then dropped off the stage." There were also hints that Providence had been wise in removing so swiftly someone whose naïveté and ignorance of world affairs had already got him into trouble.

Perhaps his worst mistake was to receive General Videla, president of Argentina, without realizing that this would be badly received by Latin American Catholics, who were preparing their Puebla meeting where they hoped to deliver a salutary shock to military dictators with their theory of the "national security state." On the other hand, Cardinal Joseph Ratzinger, archbishop of Munich, warned the conclave that it would be under intense pressure to go for a candidate who favored an "opening to the left" or the "historic compromise" with the Communists, and that this should be resisted. John Paul I had been critical of liberation theology, and that tradition should be continued by the next pope.

On October 15, 111 cardinals went into the conclave. For the first time in history, the number of non-European cardinals (56) exceeded that of European (55). Of the non-Europeans, 19 were Latin Americans, 13 North Americans, 12 Africans, 9 Asians, and 4 from Oceania. There were still 26 Italians. Little is known of the dynamics of this conclave. Certainly there was drama, hinted at in the remark of Cardinal Enrique y Tarancón: "God made use of human malignity and of divisions among the Italians."

Who were the competing Italians who knocked one another out? According to Siri's secretary, "Cardinal Siri lacked only a few votes to obtain the required majority. Not more than four or five."[10] This source, admittedly too close to be entirely reliable, also asserts that Siri would have been pope had he been willing to envisage Cardinal Giovanni Benelli of Florence as his secretary of state—which he was not prepared to do. The four ballots of the first day did not produce a solution. Siri was the candidate of reaction and

Benelli of openness to the world. But though they came close, neither could reach the required majority.

A variety of factors conspired to propel Karol Wojtyla through the gap this left. The first was that the conclave had run out of pastoral-minded Italians of sufficient caliber. Therefore there was an opening for a non-Italian. Wyszynski's paper at the August conclave suggested that if a "strong doctrinal pope" were needed, then Eastern Europe could provide one. Moreover, after the death of John Paul I, physical fitness was essential, a young fifty-eight-year-old who skied and climbed mountains would fit the bill. Again, Wojtyla had been elected to the council of the synod in 1971—it had only twelve elected members—and he was very active in promoting its work. Cardinal Sebastiano Baggio, head of the Congregation of Bishops, set him up to give the position papers at the synod of 1974 on evangelization. Wojtyla dealt very satisfactorily in Baggio's view with the drift to liberation theology. Wojtyla was, in fact, better known than Luciani. Was Baggio his *grande elettore?*

There was something very special about this conclave. Something unusual and unprecedented happened. Cardinal John J. Carberry, the harmonica-playing archbishop of St. Louis, said, typically, "I would like to tell you everything. It would thrill you. But I can't." Cardinal Siri told Benny Lai that it would be a good thing—some time in the future—to tell how this conclave went. "For secrecy," he said darkly, "though valid at the time of the conclave, can cover over some very uncharitable actions."[11] Karol Wojtyla, after his election, remarked that electing him showed "great courage."

Now there is a theory that meets these requirements. By Sunday evening, the conclave mood was rather depressed. No one was seriously emerging. They could spend a lot of time trying out candidates who manifestly could not rally the necessary support, but that would mean going around in circles. At this point, Cardinal Franz König of Vienna, supported by Cardinal Joseph Ratzinger (it is alleged) suggested a departure from precedent. Instead of allowing the conclave to be dominated by unavowed "factions" or "parties," could they not try out, as a way of resolving the impasse, a really surprise candidate like Karol Wojtyla? His merits were known. He could bring the vigor of the East to the rather tired West. His Italian was excellent.[12]

Once the idea was proposed, it gained ground rapidly until, by lunchtime the following day, Wojtyla was ahead and by the eighth ballot elected. A kind of confirmation was conveyed by the remark of Cardinal Hyacynthe Thiandoum, archbishop of Dakar, who said, "We were surprised by the emergence of this candidate. If his name had emerged on the first day, everything would have gone more swiftly."

Another detail, from another source, completes the picture. Cardinal Giovanni Colombo, who succeeded Paul VI in Milan and was his confidant, refused to be considered as a candidate. At seventy-six he felt too old (though that was the age at which John XXIII was elected). He added a "revelation." Paul VI believed that a man of seventy-five would rarely be capable of keeping up with the demands of the modern papacy. He considered resigning himself but was talked out of it. He did not wish to create a precedent such that every pope, on reaching seventy-five, would *have to* resign, but he wanted the conclave to know his judgment that if a pope felt unable to continue after seventy-five, he should be free to resign without feeling he was setting a precedent.

This remark was made at the August conclave of 1978, but it became more relevant than ever in the October conclave. It meant the cardinals could elect a fifty-eight-year-old pope without committing themselves to an immensely long pontificate. So Cardinal Karol Wojtyla became pope on October 16, 1978. After toying with the name Stanislaus, he opted for the safer course of Pope John Paul II, which the Roman crowd practically imposed on him. His pontificate of surprises began with the biggest surprise of all: his election.

One important postscript to this chapter is needed. The surroundings everyone suffered in 1978 may change by the time of the next conclave. In 1993, work began on a new hotel-like building on the Piazza Santa Marta just inside the Vatican to the left of St. Peter's. It will cost $15 million and is said to have been provided by United States benefactors—most probably the Knights of Columbus, who previously paid for the refurbishing of the Vatican press office.

Officially the purpose of the new building is to house long-term guests to Rome. But with its 130 rooms "complete with every amenity," it could well be used for the next conclave. The building will be ready by 1996. The Italian Green party piously objected that it would block the view of the dome of St. Peter's from the Via di Porta Caval-leggieri, so the top floor was lopped off the plans and a half-basement substituted.

Many said that the uncomfortable surroundings in 1978 made for undue haste. In their new comfortable setting, equivalent to a five-star hotel, the cardinals could work at leisure. There is just one problem: how to get them back and forth to the Sistine Chapel twice a day without breach-ing security. Various suggestions have been made: an un-derground corridor or a sealed private passageway through St. Peter's are possible answers.

Some thought has been given to the possibility of hold-ing the conclave in a wing of St. Peter's, such as the nave of St. Joseph. Paul VI's regulations allow for that. Article 39 says, "All the cardinal electors summoned ... to elect the pontiff are bound in virtue of holy obedience to give their assent to the summons and proceed to the place designated for the elections." It could be the end for the newly cleansed Sistine Chapel.

FOUR The Polish Factor

So John Paul II was—by a quirk of fate, by the careful planning of Cardinal Baggio, by the intervention of Cardinal König, or by the operations of Divine Providence—unexpectedly elected pope on October 16, 1978.

There is a great difficulty in speaking honestly and directly about popes, for as soon as a man becomes pope a process of mythologization sets in that transforms overnight the mediocre into a genius and the merely talented into a superluminary. No one—outside the narrow circle of phenomenologists—had paid much attention to the philosophical work of Karol Wojtyla.

Yet once he became pope, *The Acting Person* was translated into the main European languages; and the Catholic University of Lublin, which had isolated him when he was teaching there, began the intensive study of his works, as though he were, as they soon claimed, "one of the greatest thinkers of the twentieth century." Such assertions look patently absurd once the pope is dead, but while he is alive they combine with "creeping infallibility" to make any criticism difficult. The pope, as Vatican I says clearly, is endowed only with "that infallibility with which the Church is endowed" and can exercise his charisma of infallibility only in exceptional situations. There has been only one such occasion since 1870: the definition of the Assumption of 1950. But a kind of spectral aura or penumbra of infallibility comes to envelop the pope's every utterance. I have heard Pope John Paul exhort the Cagliari soccer team to attend carefully to the (his) ordinary *magisterium*. To little avail.

The problem is compounded in a pope who has such a clear sense of his providential mission. What is the providential meaning of this controversial pontificate? This is not a question that a historian or observer can tackle with any confidence. The college of cardinals, however, is the least likely body in the Church to fall into these traps. The cardinals do not mythologize the talents of the present pope or overestimate his importance as a philosopher. They will not have an exaggerated respect for his ordinary *magisterium*, because it has tended to eclipse, most unjustly, their own. They can speak their minds. "It is not the best of [his] encyclicals," confessed Belgian cardinal Godfried Danneels of *Veritatis Splendor,* "but it is an important document."[1] As for judging the providential meaning of the pontificate, they are no better placed than anyone else.

So the analysis of the recent pontificate in the college of cardinals will be hardheaded and frank. Because it will take place in private, no punches need be pulled. And though the majority of the cardinals will have been chosen by the recently deceased pope, that does not mean that they will be in excessive awe of him or unable to think dispassionately about his pontificate.

This chapter will consider one aspect of the inheritance of Pope John Paul II, as it will appear after his death. The next conclave will have one feature that no conclave has ever had before: never before has there been a conclave after a *Polish* pope. One sure thing is that another Polish pope will not emerge, not only because none of the Polish cardinals have enough stature, but because it would suggest a Polish takeover. One Polish pope is quite enough for a century or so. A Roman joke says that the mysterious third secret of Fátima is "Repent and pray—or you will have another Polish pope." One aspect of the analysis of the pontificate will be to determine what *Polish* features it possesses, for they will obviously not be repeatable.

So the old question asked on the eve of every conclave—continuity or discontinuity?—will be asked in a new form. The difficulty lies in sorting out what is particularly Polish from what is generally conservative. For example, is Pope John Paul's partiality for Opus Dei to be attributed to his Polishness or his conservatism? There can be no doubt about the fact of his partiality. The contrast is very marked between his attitude toward Opus Dei and toward the great religious orders like the Jesuits, the Dominicans, and the Franciscans, all of whom have been were shabbily treated. His affection for Opus Dei was strong enough for him to allow the beatification of Josémaria Escrivá despite well-founded protests and obvious irregularities. Was that part of being Polish, or of being conservative?

In a rare interview in late 1993 Pope John Paul was asked by Jas Gawronski what difference being Polish made to his pontificate. The second part of his answer was rather surprising:

> *I grew up there, and therefore have brought with me the history, the culture, the experience and the language of Poland. Even now when I write something, I write it in Polish.*
>
> *Having lived in a country which had to struggle for its freedom, in a country vulnerable to the aggression and dictates of its neighbors, I have been led to sympathize with the plight of the countries of the Third World, which also are subject to another type of dependence, the economic one. . . . I have understood what exploitation is, and I have sided unequivocally with the poor, with the disinherited, the oppressed, the marginalized and the defenseless.* [2]

This statement is touching in its disingenuousness. His friends in Opus Dei are hardly noted for their love of the church of the poor. Yet the succession matters more to Opus Dei than to any other group in the Church. Having enjoyed the favor of the prince, they cannot expect that to continue into the next pontificate.

This is only one example of how the question of continuity or discontinuity will arise. Should the pontificate that will have just ended simply be carried on as far as possible by a clonelike disciple of John Paul II? That would be a missed opportunity.

So the conclave will begin with an analysis of the pontificate of Pope John Paul II. What inheritance will he bequeath to the Church? Judgments on this score are not lacking. "Conservatives" applaud him as the man who restored order and Catholic identity after the (as they see it) confusions and vacillations of Pope Paul VI. "Liberals" deplore him as the man who restored the monarchical papacy, undermined the collegiality of the bishops proclaimed by Vatican II, and while "saving" the Church in central and Eastern Europe, antagonized theologians, and by attacking liberation theology risked losing the Church in Latin America. God-like objectivity is impossible in such matters. What is at stake is not what any individual thinks about the pontificate but how the college of cardinals will judge it when it is over.

One of the key moments in Pope John Paul's pontificate came on his return to Poland in June 1979, within a year of his election. The first non-Italian pope for 455 years happened to be a Slav. When he met Mikhail Gorbachev in December 1991, the Soviet president congratulated him on being the first Polish pope. John Paul gently corrected him: "The first Slav pope." "But you are a West Slav," said Gorbachev. "It is the same," said John Paul, thus casting his spell over Gorbachev and drawing him within his pastoral orbit. If there really was a "common European home," as Gorbachev had announced in Prague in 1987, then only the pope could welcome him into it.

But that was "future music" when Pope John Paul stood before a million well-disciplined and orderly people in Victory Square, Warsaw, on Saturday, June 2, 1979, the eve of Pentecost. It was an extraordinary event. In the heart of a Communist capital, Warsaw—a stone's throw away from the tomb of the Polish unknown soldier, whose battles began in the Middle Ages—a huge cross was erected. It was dismantled before sunset that same day. The pope ended his homily with these words: "Come Holy Spirit, fill the hearts of the faithful and renew the face of the earth." But then he added, with a sweeping gesture, "of this earth." The Polish word for earth *(ziemen)* also means land or country. In other words, he was beseeching the Holy Spirit to liberate Poland. This was no mere rhetorical flourish.

No pope has thought more, or at any rate written more, about Europe than John Paul II. A book published in 1989 analyzed 55 speeches on European questions.[3] The complete collection up to August 26, 1991, comprises 285 items.[4] Speeches and addresses have not grown fewer since then. It would not be unreasonable to speak of an obsession with Europe. But his image of Europe, his *Europabild*, is not one to which most of us are accustomed. It is in some ways rather disconcerting. It is always Europe seen from Poland.

His first major address on Europe came from Gniezno, the Canterbury of Poland, where the earliest Polish kings were buried and which boasts the shrine of Saint Adalbert. Here occurred in 966 the founding act of the Polish Church: the baptism of Miesko I. History for John Paul is a storehouse of powerful images. Every May 3 he went to Gniezno for the feast of St. Adalbert, which is also known as Constitution Day after the first Polish Constitution of 1791.

The point was crystal clear. In Poland no wedge can be driven between conversion to Christianity and establishment of the nation: they were one and the same event. *Chrzest*, the Polish word for baptism, is more like our word *christen*. This is why the pope so often uses formulas like "France, remember your baptism" and why "de-Christianization" for him represents apostasy. In Poland in 1979 he proclaimed the "spiritual unity" of Europe at a time when the continent was still physically divided by the iron curtain. He declared, in effect, the division of Europe anomalous and its frontiers irrelevant. In Poland he acted as a "tribune of the people," articulating what was felt but could not be said. That gave the Polish workers enough self-confidence to found Solidarity. But Poland's "vocation" depended on the "founding act" of 966.

John Paul applies this notion elsewhere. He saw Columbus's "discovery" of America in 1492 as another founding act, the beginning of evangelization and civilization, interchangeable terms. Within that framework are other founding acts, such as the moment the cross was planted on the shore of Vera Cruz, and when Brazil came into existence on May 3, 1500, feast of Holy Cross. But it is in Europe that the founding act of baptism is seen most vividly and has evident political implications.

The baptism of Rus in the land of Kiev in 988 was the theme of two encyclicals on its millennium. John Paul said, "We unite ourselves with all those who recognize in the baptism received by their ancestors the source of their religious, cultural and national identity."[5] This was clearly an attempt to stake a claim on the Russian Orthodox tradition, in his view equally well represented by the Ukrainian Catholic Church (or Uniate Church). Of Lithuania he said, "Christianity was the true evangelical leaven of the nation, it marked its daily life, it put down solid roots and so became, so to speak, its soul." Always there is this triad of religion-culture-nature, which are seen as inseparable.

N. B.

This was also an anticommunist motif. It was an answer to anyone naive enough to believe that history began with the "revolution" or, more improbably, with the coming of the Red Army. Communism tried to present itself as scientific and modern. In 1966 Poland celebrated its own millennium—twenty-two years before the baptism of Rus in Kiev. Throughout that year the battle for the soul of the nation raged. The question was, Where was the true national tradition of Poland expressed?

But there was another aspect of John Paul's Gniezno address in 1979. These were early days in which he pinched himself and asked why he had been elected pope. What was the providential meaning of his pontificate? What was God trying to say through his election? Most of us would be loath to answer such a question very precisely: who can scrutinize the ways of the Lord? But John Paul's answer was very clear. He had been chosen as pope to bring to the whole Church community the special contribution of the Slav peoples to Europe in particular:

> *Does not Christ wish to hear . . . with special understanding, special sensitivity, those sounds of human speech which are in-*

*terlinked in a common root, a common etymology and which
... sound so close to each other? Is not the Holy Spirit dis-
posed to see that this Polish pope, this Slav pope, should at
this very moment reveal the spiritual unity of Europe?*[26]

This hint at the providential meaning of his election was
couched in the form of rhetorical questions, but that modesty takes away none of its force.

In Gniezno, John Paul was not just the heir of the Polish national tradition, with its religious and cultural dimen-
sions. From there he proclaimed the "spiritual unity of Europe" not as some kind of task to be realized but as an
already accomplished fact. Europe, still in 1979 manifestly
divided by the iron curtain, by ideological opposition, and
by threatening military alliances, was "spiritually united."

Did this mean united in the mind? Was the spiritual
unity of Europe just "something that goes on in the head"?
Was it the kind of "idealism" for which Marxists habitually
had such contempt?

For the pope, the word *spiritual,* far from meaning un-
real, means what is most really real. Compared with the centuries of shared European history, the forty or so years since
Yalta divided Europe were a mere blink, a temporary aberra-
tion. It followed that the divisions of Europe were man-
made, artificial, and therefore doomed. It's easy enough to
see that now, and even to regard it as a truism, but in 1979 it
was a bold and very challenging claim.

Six years later, another Slav reached the same conclusion:

*Scanning the panorama of this long suffering land and pon-
dering on the common roots of such a multi-form but essentially common European civilization, I felt with growing
acuteness the artificiality and temporariness of the bloc-to-bloc
confrontation, and the archaic nature of the "iron curtain."*[7]

The assertion of the "spiritual unity" of Europe, echoed by
Gorbachev, stands Marxism on its head. It is an instance of
the spiritual shaping, determining, and leading the material. *Primus concepit mente.* Get the thinking right first.

If one asked in 1979 just what was being united, the
pope's answer would be peoples first and then, perhaps,
nations. He needed this distinction because throughout
the nineteenth century Poland was carved up among its
three powerful neighbors, Austria, Prussia, and Russia. His
father—he pointed out—was no less Polish for having an
Austrian passport and serving in the Austro-Hungarian
army.

But to be spiritually united means nothing unless there
are real exchanges. Though the frontiers of Europe could
not be totally ignored in the 1980s, they were increasingly
disregarded or regarded as anomalous, so much so that
when they crumbled late in 1989, people wondered why
the dogs, the mines and trip-wires, and the border shoot-
ings had ever existed.

John Paul's image of Europe included a vision—there
is no other word for it—of a Europe without frontiers
through which people wander freely. But they wander pur-
posefully. They go on pilgrimages. For the pope the key
pilgrimage center that forged European awareness was San-

tiago de Compostela. Here is what he said about it in the autumn of 1982:

In the centuries when a homogeneous and spiritually united continent was being shaped, the whole of Europe came here to the "memorial" of Saint James. It was one of the places that favored the mutual understanding of the so very different European peoples, the Latins, the Germans, the Celts, the Anglo-Saxons, and the Slavs. The pilgrimage brought together, put in contact and united all those peoples who throughout the centuries, once touched by the preaching of Christ's apostles, accepted the Gospel, and at the same time were born as peoples and nations.[8]

So it's not just the nations, it is Europe itself that is baptized and acquires its identity through its baptism.

This is a highly sacralized view of the continent. The pope's map of Europe is very special and selective. It doesn't include steel factories or power stations or computer-based industries; it marks Marian pilgrimage centers and Czestochowa, Velherad, Lourdes, Knock, and shrines connected with the local saints. This sacred Euro-map is superimposed upon the ordinary map. Everything that is not directly linked to the fundamental vision is omitted.

Protestants like Luther and Calvin are excluded. Even the Catholic Erasmus did not rate a mention on the visit to the Netherlands. If these fellow Christians cannot edge their way in, then there is no hope at all for the secular *N B.* thinkers who have made their mark on Europe. It is true that John Paul did mention Goethe at Compostela, but only to say that Goethe suggested that "European awareness" was born on pilgrimage. Secular thinkers are allowed to re-inforce, but not to challenge, the main vision.

This sacralized Europe cuts clean across the ordinary perception of Europe as to some extent post-Christian. John Paul's vision doesn't fit the realities of the Europe we actually experience. He cheerfully accepts that his message challenges the conventional wisdom, is a sign of contradiction (title of one of his books), and flings down the gauntlet to contemporary Europe. He doesn't mind that at all. He loves a scrap.

Perhaps the reason he prefers Compostela to Rome itself is that it developed as the Moors—the Muslims—had been driven out of Spain. It fits the crusading spirit better. Its intellectual world is the first European epic, the *Song of Roland*, in which *Chrestiens unt raison, paiens unt tort* (the Christians are right, and the pagans are wrong). The solemn rhetoric of Compostela is all devoted to a rediscovery. The re- prefixes abound: "I bishop of Rome and pastor of the universal church, from Saint James of Compostela, send my cry of love toward you, old Europe. Rediscover yourself, be yourself. Revivify your roots. Relive the authentic values that have been the glory of your history." Was it a restoration he has in mind? Does he dream of a new Christendom in which there would be an overlap, a perfect fit, between religious and social life? He hasn't used the term, and it seems an impossible dream.

Yet something analogous is implied by all the talk of a "second evangelization" of Europe that has been such a feature of the pontificate. It is addressed to the young in particular. He appeals to them "to bring about a second evangelization of European society by your effective commitment. That's a task that belongs to young people especially and challenges them. The 'refoundation' of European culture is the most decisive and urgent enterprise of our time."[9] This project, whatever it really means, is concerned with European *society*.

There is in the pope no privatization of Christian faith, hope, or charity. He wants them all to be embodied in the structures of society, and this is the primary task of laypeople. But the reverse of this particular medal is that making an impact on society also means refusing the distinction between law and morality. It means in practice that the pope has no use for pluralism, and that he would ideally like legislation to reflect Catholic moral teaching whether Catholics are in a majority or not. So "bringing the second evangelization to European society" really means mobilizing people, especially young people, for a series of moral campaigns.

N B

Equipped with this image of Europe, Pope John Paul has never liked the way the European Union (né Community) made off with the adjective *European*. Neither the European Commission nor the European Parliament to which it is supposedly accountable display a broad enough concept of Europe for him. Their attempts, after Maastricht, to conduct a coherent foreign policy seem to him derisory; Europe's sad incapacity to put a stop to the tragedy of the former Yugoslavia suggests that he is not wholly wrong.

There is a paradox here. His Europe is a Europe of peoples, of nations, and it stretches like Charles de Gaulle's Europe from the Atlantic to the Urals. He attaches so much importance to the baptism of Rus because it permits him to get, roughly, to the Urals. And that marks the easternmost point of penetration of Christianity into Asia. But if the nations, and consequently nationalism in some form or another, played their part in the overthrow of Communism, they have also played a role in post-Communist chaos.

Addressing the CSCE (Conference on Security and Co-operation in Europe) in November 1993, he welcomed the new nations back to the map. But he warned that things would go badly wrong if "a falsely united multinational society" (translation, the Soviet Union and its satellites) should now be succeeded by "one falsely diversified" (in other words, the Baltic republics should treat their Russians nicely).[10]

John Paul counts Russia conditionally as part of "our common European home." In the last article he wrote before becoming pope, he inquired where the easternmost border of Europe was to be found. It was not on any map: it occurred where the Christian emphasis on the dignity of the individual human person met the enslavement and tyranny that came from the East.

So one of John Paul's first acts as pope was to proclaim Saints Cyril and Methodius co-equal patrons of Europe alongside Saint Benedict. Paul VI had declared Benedict patron of Europe in 1964. Had he been falling down on the job? No, that was not the point. By setting the two brothers from Salonika and apostles of the Slavs alongside Saint Benedict of Nursia, John Paul was correcting what he saw as a historic imbalance between West and East.

He was also trying to right a profound historical injustice. Poles resented that the Eastern, and specifically the Slav, contribution to the universal Church had not been properly recognized. There was a factor of compensation at work in making Cyril and Methodius co-patrons of Europe. Poles had been smarting for a long time under their inability to make themselves understood. Now I will show you, he said in effect.

Benedictine monasticism is fine, but it is too closely associated with Western Europe. Cyril and Methodius represent the "wider Europe" before the divisions of East and West occurred. They are presented as precursors of ecumenism and models of evangelization today because they translated the Gospels into the language and customs of the Slav peoples (nos. 14 and 21). *Slavorum Apostoli* was the first encyclical devoted to Europe.

Moreover, and this is another constant theme, the Church needs both traditions just as the body needs two lungs to breathe—the "Latin" tradition, which is rational, juridical, practical, needs filling out by the Oriental tradition, which is more mystical, intuitive, and charismatic (in the sense of being led by the Holy Spirit).

The greater part of the *magisterium* of Pope John Paul can be read as a way of trying to bring to the West this wisdom of the East. For example, the encyclical on suffering, *Salvifici Doloris* (February 11, 1984), is a reproach to Western superficiality for failing to grapple with the reality of evil in a century that has known "an incomparable accumulation of sufferings, even to the possible self-destruction of the planet" (8). In this dramatic and apocalyptic view, to be talking about birth control or women priests seems intolerably shallow.

Western Europeans are accustomed to thinking of themselves as on center stage, no doubt presumptuously. John Paul simply moved the center stage eastward to Warsaw. In June 1987 he stood before the Palace of Culture, that embarrassing building Stalin gave as a gift to the people of Warsaw. (He made them pay for it, and it is now, ironically enough, the Stock Exchange). Looking eastward with his back to the building, John Paul sketched out his vision of the universal Church: "The Church which is in Lithuania, Belorussia, in Ukraine, in Kiev and in the territories of Great Russia and of our brother Slavs (and also the non-Slavs), to the south in the countries once visited by the saintly brothers Cyril and Methodius." This is what happens when you look eastward, with a side glance at the Balkans. The rest of the map was quickly filled in: "And in all of Europe. In the American continents that are preparing to celebrate the 500th anniversary of their evangelization. In Africa, Australia, and Asia, and in all the islands and archipelagoes of all the seas and oceans." It is always chastening to be put firmly in one's place, and a new experience for Western Europeans to be relegated to "the rest of Europe."

In this picture of the world, Western Europe stands behind the pope, at his shoulder, as it were, and that is why it needs its "second evangelization." It has to be disciplined and well ordered, marshaled and in line. The appointments of conservative bishops and the curbs on theologians are seen as part of this process: it is a matter of getting the troops in line.

Such thoughts are not just an exhortation for internal Church use—still less, pulpit rhetoric. When he had an opportunity in October 1988 to address the most representative elected body in Europe, the European Parliament, John Paul did not change or adapt his language to the circumstances. Far from it, he struck a blow at the very basis of its tolerance of pluralism. When, he said, all subordination of the creature to God and all reference to a transcendent order of truth and goodness are excluded, man is made the measure of all things. What happens then? "Ethics then has no foundation other than social consensus, and individual liberty has no brake other than what society thinks it must impose for the safeguard of others."[11] That describes the practical, workaday ethics on which pluralist societies like ours do in fact have to operate.

In Strasbourg the pope warned about the "somber perspectives" that would open up for all Europeans if God were eased out of public life. Why is this so dangerous? Because the "supreme guarantee against all abuses of power by man over man" would no longer be available. It is very attractive to think of God as saving us from the idolatry of the state or a dictator like Stalin, and that is part of Pope John Paul's own Polish experience. But it is possible to think that the separation of powers between the executive, the legislative, and the judiciary is another more earthbound guarantee against tyranny that can also come in useful. But the pope did not present his views as something to be debated. He was Cassandra, warning of catastrophe.

John Paul's anticommunist crusade succeeded. Beyond his dreams. Beyond anyone's dreams. The encyclical *Centesimus Annus*, published in 1991 on the hundredth anniversary of Leo XIII's social encyclical *Rerum Novarum*, celebrated this victory. It included a paean to democracy such as had not been seen before: "The Church values the democratic system inasmuch as it ensures the participation of citizens in making political choices, guarantees to the governed the possibility both of electing and holding accountable those who govern them, and of replacing them through peaceful means where appropriate."(46) This reflected the Polish experience, in which democracy appeared as the only peaceable alternative to totalitarian rule. Lezsek Kolakowski's question remained hanging in the air: Did the Church in Poland oppose Communism because it was totalitarian or because it was anti-God?

If the dramatic liberation from Communism was, as Cardinal Józef Glemp said, like the crossing of the Red Sea by the people of Israel, since then there has been much floundering about in the desert, cries for more manna, and murmurings against Moses. Does this mean that the commitment to democracy has been weakened?

Yes and no. There is a nuance. In his most recent encyclical, *Veritatis Splendor*, Pope John Paul warns against "the risk of an alliance between democracy and ethical relativism, which would remove any sure moral reference points from political and social life" (101). He then quotes another passage from *Centesimus Annus*, which was overlooked in the residual euphoria of 1991: "As history demonstrates, a democracy without values easily turns into open or thinly disguised totalitarianism."

Unfortunately no examples of this historical process are provided, so it is difficult to know exactly what this means. But the pope's speech to intellectuals in Riga, Latvia, suggests that "liberalism," understood as the ideological underpinning of capitalism, has replaced Communism as the new "enemy."

Yet in Riga for the first time ever he admitted that Marxism possessed "a kernel of truth." Marxism rightly recognized, he said, "the situation of exploitation to which an inhumane capitalism has subjected the proletariat since the beginning of industrialized society." But it was destined to fail, since it has a wrong understanding of the human person. Capitalism will fail for the same reason. "There are many human needs which find no place on the market," as *Centesimus Annus* noted (34).

Western thinkers have established a strong link between capitalism and democracy, between the freedom of the market and the freedom to vote. If the pope is right in seeing a link between "democracy and ethical relativism," then the outlook for democracy in Africa and Eastern Europe is bleak, and the position of Catholics in pluralist democracies is put in jeopardy. The pope is tempted by theocracy.

Jerzy Turowicz, veteran editor of *Tygodnik Powszechny*, the Kraków Catholic weekly, has known the pope as a friend since 1949 and is a lucid and courageous man. In 1990 he wrote an editorial entitled "Where we come from and where we are going":

There are people who think that totalitarianism in the service of a false ideology is wrong, whereas when in the service of a correct and true ideology it is good. That is false. Catholicism (and Christianity too) is not an ideology, and every totalitarianism is wrong. . . . The state is the common property of all citizens, irrespective of their confession, nationality or convictions. Poland it not the exclusive property of Catholics, no matter how numerous they may be. The slogan "To be Polish is to be Catholic" has a good meaning when it indicates the bond of this nation with the faith of the Church. But it is bad when it serves to divide people or treat people of other confessions or unbelievers as second-class citizens. . . . Catholics do not have the right to compel others to accept their convictions.[12]

This wisdom from a Polish Catholic layman will be followed by the next pope. The Church has to learn to live in a pluralist society. One cannot, as we move into the twenty-first century, count on authoritarian regimes exercising a theocracy, even a benevolent one.

However, everything so far said in this chapter will appear unbearably Euro-centric to some Asians, Latin Americans, and Africans. They will be disappointed to learn that "liberalism" has replaced "Communism" as the target of the pope's crusade. The whole discussion remains locked in a time warp in which the most important events are the Reformation and the eighteenth-century Enlightenment. For non-Europeans (and for Europeans too, did they but know it), the North-South divide has replaced the East-

West preoccupation; and the North is rich and well fed, while the South is poor and hungry.

This is the most important challenge to be faced by the world and consequently the Church at the end of the twentieth century. The *Human Development Report* of 1992 pictures on its cover a champagne glass—a wide, shallow bowl atop a slender stem. The billion people who live in the industrialized nations are the champagne people, less than a fifth of the world's population yet with more than four-fifths of the world's income. In this perspective the spread of democracy in recent years, though welcome, leaves untouched the realm of poverty, where access "to the ordinary opportunities of life—land, water, work, living space, and basic social services"—is all the time shrinking. Hence the conclusion: "Some people claim that recent events prove the triumph of capitalism and the demise of socialism. This is too simplistic a view. If there is a triumph of capitalism, it need not be a triumph of greed. If there is a demise of socialism, it need not be the demise of all social objectives." This is not so very different from what Pope John Paul himself said in Riga, addressing Latvian intellectuals. But he did not put it in a North-South context.

The next pontificate will see the world in those terms. From this point of view, the pontificate of Pope John Paul II will appear to history as a Polish interlude. It is exciting, heroic, and exceptional (in the sense of an *état d'exception*), and after it a more mundane and feet-on-the-ground papacy will be desirable.

I know it is a myth, but the image that springs to mind is of the chivalrous Polish knight on a white charger who fearlessly tackles the panzers of the modern world and perishes in the attempt to reverse the secular course of European history. But if it is a failure, it a noble and heroic one, grandiose in its scope and aims.

FIVE

The Conclave Agenda

The Polish perspective on Europe and the world is the main key that unlocks the meaning of Pope John Paul II's pontificate. But it is not the only one. The Second Vatican Council (1962–65) remains the most epoch-making event in the life of the Catholic Church in the twentieth century. The pontificate of Paul VI was a conscious attempt to implement Vatican II and to bring out the "spiritual dialectic" that underpinned it. The question naturally arises, What was Pope John Paul's attitude to Vatican II?

On his election he declared that the full implementation of Vatican II would be the program of his pontificate. Was that really true? Before the conclave begins, during the *Novemdiales*, the conclave will have to decide how the pontificate that just ended really stands in regard to Vatican II. It will not regard lip service as sufficient.

"Actions speak louder than words" can be applied to John Paul's pontificate. Though Paul VI has been lavishly praised as "our venerable predecessor," he is presented as a tragic figure who couldn't quite cope. John Paul's actions say clearly that he considers Paul VI to have been weak and vacillating, if not utterly mistaken on priestly identity, religious life, dangerous theologians, episcopal collegiality, ecumenism, and Vatican II itself. In his judgment, Paul VI was too lenient in his treatment of allegedly dissident theologians, did not push hard enough on *Humanae Vitae,* surrendered Catholic identity in his ecumenical enthusiasm, and failed to show sufficient firmness in dealing with the Jesuits and other religious orders, especially women's religious orders already infected with "feminism."

The Extraordinary Synod of 1985, with its abandonment of "the People of God" as the key concept for the understanding of the Church and its "pessimistic" re-editing of the "signs of the times," confirmed that Paul VI's interpretation of Vatican II was being rejected. This is grave, because what I am calling "Paul VI's interpretation of Vatican II" was the standard view shared by bishops, priests, theologians, and Christians generally.

There is a paradox here. No doubt John Paul II was sincere in his proclamations of fidelity to Vatican II, but he was committed to Vatican II as interpreted in a highly idiosyncratic way. This is another instance of the highly personal nature of this pontificate.

A Polish theologian, and his student and friend, Halina Bortnowska, introduced the Italian edition of his book on the Council, *Sources of Renewal,* in this way: *"Sources of Renewal* was a first provisional sketch. The author hides behind numerous quotations from the Council. . . . The Council texts and they alone occupy the stage and there is no appeal to postconciliar discussions. One has a feeling of great abstractness and remoteness from the world of people seeking some guidance for their lives."[1]

Thus, while theologians in the West were interpreting the council as an innovation, Karol Wojtyla saw it as an unruffled confirmation of traditional views. It did not generate excitement or any great hope for the renewal of the Church or involve participation of the laity. He saw it as a private spiritual experience of the bishops who took part in it. So there was a basic misunderstanding between Poland and the rest of the developed world on what the council really meant.

The failed assassination attempt in 1981 confirmed John Paul in his personal approach to the pontificate. Some might call it a messianistic approach. He certainly feels that having Providence on his side, he has something to teach the whole Church. The principal effect was that he no longer needed to listen to any advice within the Church and could concentrate on his personal agenda. Time and time again, he warned that "the Church is not a democracy" and castigated the abusive exploitation of the idea of the Church as "the People of God." *Veritatis Splendor* provides a classic statement of this view: "While exchanges and conflicts of opinion may constitute normal expressions of public life in a representative democracy, moral teaching cannot depend upon respect for a process; indeed, it is in no way established by following the rules and deliberative principles typical of a democracy" (113). The point is well made. The Church is not a democracy. Doctrinal and moral decisions are not arrived at by a majority vote or counting heads.

But, as the prophetic figure of Pedro Casaldáliga, bishop of Sao Felix, Brazil, remarked, "The Church is not a democracy, sure. I don't want the Church to be a democracy. I want it to be something better than a democracy. I want it to be a community." A prophet speaking. Casaldáliga was reproached for not going on the *ad limina* visits to the pope that bishops must make every five years. Finally, after seventeen years, he made it to Rome in 1988. He was interrogated about his views on liberation theology by Cardinal Bernardin Gantin. "You said that *ad limina* visits were useless," Gantin complained. Casaldáliga corrected him: "Almost useless."

When he got to see Pope John Paul—for fifteen minutes—they discussed a future visit to Brazil. Casaldáliga suggested that Gantin's desire to have his replies in writing suggested a lack of trust. "It can also be a sign of confidence," John Paul replied. "Cardinal Paulo Evaristo Arns when he comes here likes to have things in writing." Then the pope sat down, opened his arms, and "half-jesting and half-warning" explained: "So that you may see I am no wild beast." Casaldáliga did not know what to make of this.

But he was right in thinking that the truism that "the Church is not a democracy" was used to eliminate not only all dissent but all serious consultation in the Church. All the organs of consultation set in place by Vatican II were one by one emasculated. The Synod of Bishops, which was intended to continue the collegiality or team spirit among all the world's bishops, was turned into a rally supporting the papal theses: the high point of futility was reached at the 1990 Synod on the Priestly Ministry when the notion of ordaining married men because of acute pastoral need was rejected out of hand. Presented as a free "decision" of the synod, it was imposed on the synod by papal *fiat*.

The devaluation of the synod was only one aspect of the general undermining of episcopal or collegial authority. A study was ordered, allegedly in response to the 1985 Synod on Vatican II, on the exact theological status and nature of episcopal conferences (or local benches of bishops). It has not yet appeared.

The draft denies to episcopal conferences any theological or collegial reality, any authority to teach. Only individual bishops have such authority. When they enter the episcopal conference, they leave their authority outside, with their umbrellas and coats, in the cloakroom. But when episcopal authority is thus undermined, then *a fortiori* the laity are reduced to complete passivity, growling impotence, and silent fury.

Pope John Paul II seems utterly unaware of what he has done to the credibility of the Church. He cannot grasp the truth contained in the bitter criticism of the Oxford zoologist, Richard Dawkins, a professional anti-Christian: "Pope John Paul II is a courageous man of rocklike character. . . . He heroically epitomizes the preposterous institution of which he is head. He is perfectly poised to do it the greatest possible damage and is in the strongest strategic position to do so. Long may he live."[2] The irony is that Pope John Paul's intransigence supplies weapons to the enemies of the Church—the very people whom he wishes to confute.

In an exchange of letters in the *Spectator,* someone defended John Paul and *Veritatis Splendor* on the grounds that he had been professor of ethics in the Catholic University of Lublin. This brought Dawkins sneering out of New College, Oxford, once again:

> *This is no ordinary professor whose views on ethics can be accepted or rejected on his arguments. This professor wouldn't recognize an argument if it bit him. It has been internally revealed to him that he is right, and he has lately reaffirmed his infallibility and he expects—with good reason—that many millions of the poorest and most overcrowded people in the world will obey him without question whatever he says. Despite appearances, this is not a gentle smiling old duffer with a harmless penchant for kissing airport taxiways, but a dangerous world-damaging dictator.*[3]

This farrago of nonsense—there was no question of infallibility in *Veritatis Splendor*—from the man whom Paul Johnson called "the poor man's Huxley" is here to illustrate that authoritarian teaching does not impress the modern world.

John Paul is not the first pope to have ruled the Church from the extreme right—Pope Saint Pius X did the same—but his historic importance is that he is the first post–Vatican II pope to attempt this tour de force. The natural place for popes is in the middle of the ecclesial road. They must not allow their personal theological opinions to influence their judgments. Otherwise they put the unity of the Church in jeopardy. They must not define the Church too narrowly. John Paul II breaks all these rules. As the late John M. Todd, English Catholic layman and founder of the publishing house of Darton, Longman, and Todd, perceptively observed, "If Paul VI was a consensus man, who won some battles, lost some, and said publicly that he didn't know what to do about others, John Paul II finds decision-making as easy as Paul VI found it difficult."[4] Todd remarks that John Paul's courage, intelligence, sincerity, are not in doubt. Yet each time he seeks to address the modern world or his critics within the Church, he fails. Says Todd, "He merely presents one side of the argument, whether he is addressing American bishops and nuns, the Anglican Church, the married laity, world demographers of the population explosion, or others."

This, in the end, will prove to have been the Achilles heel of the pontificate. To produce one side of the argument is not good enough. It makes the message of the Church unnecessarily incredible. Pope John Paul II is a convictions pope in the sense that Margaret Thatcher was a convictions politician. As with her, you are either one of us or not one of us. To put it another way, John Paul II does not understand, appreciate, or allow for the existence of a "loyal opposition" in the Church. He seems to dwell in a world in which Lenin, quoting scripture, could say, "He who is not with me is against me." Because of that he spurned the simple task of explaining to people why what he said was right. He preferred to crush them by disciplinary measures. He made the fatal mistake of assuming that disagreement meant dissidence.

This "loyal opposition" will emerge in the next conclave. Todd mentioned the way Mikhail Gorbachev was impressed, when he met Pope John Paul in December 1989, by the similarities between the Vatican and the Kremlin: a mass of churches and secular buildings crammed within the narrow compass of a walled city-state. The Kremlin, or rather the Soviet system, collapsed because its people ceased to believe in it and because the economy failed to deliver. But that is not the Vatican's situation. Todd remarks, "Most of the Vatican's critics declare themselves passionate believers in Christianity and supporters of the Catholic tradition; and the economic structure of the Catholic Church, while having taken some knocks, for instance in the banking scandals in which the Vatican was involved, is still viable."

The Vatican is not going to go broke, if the Church bestirs itself. The gates of hell will not prevail against it, and it will survive. But what exactly does that promise mean? One can ask whether it means that the Church will triumph temporally in this world, or be enabled to withstand persecution.

Then an even more redoubtable question has to be faced: What was the providential meaning of this controversial pontificate? This is not a question that a historian or observer can tackle with any confidence. But one might say that this pontificate has demonstrated, beyond doubt, that a tough-minded, hard-nosed authoritarian papacy cannot commend itself to the modern world. The conservative option has been tried. It has failed. It is time for something different.

Let me bring in another witness beyond reproach. Norbert Werbs is auxiliary bishop of Schwerin in what was East Germany. In December 1991 Werbs addressed the European synod of bishops meeting in Rome and said:

> 1. The peoples of Europe think and feel in an increasingly democratic way. Yet our Church is hierarchically structured. We are convinced that this cannot be given up. Yet we must ask ourselves whether the hierarchical setup of the Church makes possible participation and co-responsibility of all the members of the Church. The consultation process begun by Vatican II seems to many Catholics insufficient. Are they wrong? How could this be improved?
>
> 2. In stressing the priesthood of all believers Vatican II brought out their responsibility for the life of the Church. But many Catholics feel that they are denied any influence in the important process by which bishops are named. They well understand that the bishop must be in communion with the pope. But they cannot understand many recent episcopal appointments. Does this have to be so? How could it be improved?

Two external factors make this statement highly significant. First, it came not from some dissident group or left-wing publication but from a *bishop*. Admittedly only an auxiliary bishop—and after this he will no doubt remain so—but he is a product of the system he deplores. Such men have a special witness to bear. Again, Bishop Werbs comes not from the "West," which in current mythology is deeply sunk in the morass of secularization, and therefore unreliable, but from the East, the former German Democratic Republic, where the Church is believed to have been "purified" by persecution from such "secularizing" importations.

The great motive for the overthrowing of Communism was a *yearning for freedom* from totalitarian oppression. If the Church, in its own inner life, shows that it does not share in this yearning and wishes to *restore* its own authoritarian control over society, then the "decade of evangelization" in Europe will be delivered a blow from which it cannot be expected to recover. The Church is weakened wherever it gives the impression that it is concerned primarily or only with its own institutional freedom.

This is indeed the criterion for distinguishing between preconciliar and postconciliar attitudes. In the preconciliar period, the Church (that is, the hierarchy) measured freedom in terms of its own freedoms supposedly guaranteed by concordats. If in the postconciliar setting the Church is seen as "the sacrament of salvation," then the Church (that is, the People of God) shares in all the aspirations and hopes of humanity and articulates them, including the yearning for freedom.

The appointment of bishops is a particular instance of a general problem posed inevitably in the postconciliar period: Vatican II strongly asserted certain theological principles that also contained *values;* but these values cannot take effect unless they are embodied in a *praxis,* entrenched in canon law, that expresses them as adequately as possible. To borrow a distinction from Ladislas Orsy, the Church is both contemplative and active: as a contemplative body it is *quaerens intellectum fidei* (seeking the understanding of faith); as an active body it is *quaerens aedificationem regni* (seeking the building up of the kingdom).

Any gap that opens between the contemplative vision and its translation into action, any contradiction between theology and corresponding *praxis,* creates the sense of frustration and *malaise* referred to by Orsy. He explains:

> *A good deal of what is usually described as postconciliar restlessness is really nothing else than grace-filled vision postulating action. The energy contained in the word received is seeking corresponding action. Thus, our laity have heard that they were the people of God no less than the clergy, and now— no wonder!—they are asking for a more intense sharing in the sacred mission of the Church. Never again will they be satisfied with being told—as they often are—that their vocation is to sanctify secular realities.*[5]

One sphere in which this theory could be tested was in episcopal appointments. From 1984 to 1993 European bishops were parachuted down on dioceses about which they knew nothing. They were doomed to unpopularity.

Thus Joachim Meisner was transferred from East Berlin to Cologne in December 1989. The fact that none of the 815 priests of the diocese of Cologne was deemed capable of becoming bishop and none of the existing West German bishops was thought worthy of promotion seemed like a judgment on the local church. It required an "outsider" with no experience of life in the West to rule the richest and most prestigious diocese in Germany. Moreover, the provisions of the concordat were arbitrarily set aside.

In the papal mind, these unpopular bishops were meant to "restore order" and impose discipline, often with the aid of Opus Dei. The appointment of Wolfgang Haas to the diocese of Chur in Switzerland represented the most extreme example. Swiss bishops are usually appointed by cathedral chapter election. In this case, the election was avoided by making Haas coadjutor with right of succession before his predecessor retired. This was arguably unconstitutional under Swiss law and the agreements signed with the Holy See. Guests at Haas's episcopal consecration, including the prince and princess of Liechtenstein, had to step nimbly over the bodies of protesters to make their way into the cathedral.

Haas's appointment was both an *impasse* and a *reductio ad absurdum:* the irresistible force of public opinion met an immovable obstacle—the papal determination to impose this wholly unsuitable man on Chur. In the end—and this is the only instance of a climb-down, two auxiliaries were appointed so that the work of the diocese could continue. But something has been learned. The Chur scandal was not repeated in 1994, when the Basel chapter was allowed to elect the forty-three-year-old Hansjörg Vogel.

It is to be hoped that with the Basel election the practice of appointing "hard men" will cease, for a bishop cannot achieve anything without the cooperation, willing or reluctant, of his clergy and people. The only effect of such quixotic appointments is to leave the bishop brooding on his misfortune, alone in his palace, contemplating "the folly of the cross." The other effect is to alienate the faithful—especially the most zealous and committed, from whom lay ministries will have to come if the shortage of priests is to be remedied.

Nothing I have said here will come as a startling revelation to any cardinal who has been moderately alert during the last fifteen years. But none of them will say so in public: "loyalty to the Holy Father" is paramount, especially among those he "created." They keep resolutely silent. Privately they may think otherwise, but what is off the record must remain so. Still, they have their private thoughts and are saving them up for the next conclave. That will be the right time, the *kairos*, for cardinals.

What will they say? At the very least, there will be some insistence that the next papacy display a little more modesty, be less imperialist, and let the local churches breathe. A few remarks from the newly elected bishop of Basel could set them on their way. Hansjörg Vogel, who completed a doctorate in pastoral theology in Frankfurt in 1989, invited all the people of his diocese (some one and a half million) to read the Bible more prayerfully and be aware of the pressing needs of the men and women of our time. Only thus "will we be able to understand what God is saying to us today, and to draw the pastoral consequences." The key word for him is *listening*. A parish is made up of "men and women who listen."

"Listen" *(asculta)* is the first word of the Rule of Saint Benedict. Two Benedictine abbots appointed by Paul VI—Basil Hume to Westminster and Rembert Weakland to Milwaukee—quote him as saying, "The best preparation for being a bishop is to have been a Benedictine abbot." Everything Saint Benedict's Rule says about the office of abbot applies to the bishop, and also to the pope. It is, in effect, a treatise on authority in the Church. Its purpose is the service of unity. Its method is to listen to all, including the most junior members, before deciding. The art of government is so to arrange things that "while the strong have something to strive for, the weak are not crushed." It may also be relevant that Benedictine abbots are *elected* without anyone complaining of democracy's invading the Church. These two have been as successful in their dioceses as is reasonable to expect, confirming the wisdom of Saint Benedict's Rule. But that is by the way. Hume is a cardinal. Weakland is not.

The best place to observe cardinals is away from home and away from Rome. By good fortune, and courtesy of the Israeli government, in February 1994 I went to Jerusalem for a conference, "Religious Leadership in Secular Society." Among the Catholic speakers were Cardinals Joseph Ratzinger and Carlo Maria Martini. Both of them made remarkable speeches that could have a bearing on the conclave. Oddly enough, Ratzinger had chosen, or was chosen, to speak on the theme Martini is an expert on: the relations between the first covenant with the Jews and the second covenant with Christians.

Everything I said earlier about Pope John Paul's personal interpretation of Vatican II is true. But it is incomplete. The same Polish perspective that in so many ways is limiting proves liberating when one considers the relationship between Christian and Jews. No doubt the presence of Auschwitz on Polish soil made John Paul particularly sensitive on this issue. Thomas Keneally's novel *Schindler's Ark* (*Schindler's List* in the Spielberg film version), recalls the wartime Kraków he knew so well.

In *Nostra Aetate* the council rejected anti-Semitism and exculpated the Jews from "deicide." But John Paul has gone much further than any of his predecessors in providing the basis for a new understanding between Christians and Jews. He was the first pope ever to visit the Rome synagogue—there has been a synagogue in Rome since the time of Christ—where he declared that the Jewish people were our "elder brothers."

On December 30, 1993, the Fundamental Agreement between the Holy See and Israel was signed. It paved the way for diplomatic relations, whose absence had been a matter for long-standing complaint. On April 7, 1994, he was joined by some Auschwitz survivors for a concert with works by Leonard Bernstein by the London Royal Philharmonic Orchestra. A document is in preparation accepting that the Christian "teaching of contempt" made possible the *shoah* or Holocaust. There is a chance to open up a new era in Christian-Jewish relations; the next pope will not go back on that.

But Cardinal Martini, who has declared that he would only leave Milan to retire to Jerusalem, is the master in this field. At the Jerusalem conference he was landed with the concept "religious leadership." Because the papacy is the supreme instance of religious leadership, it was difficult to avoid the impression that he was saying something about the papal office. The Italian press has already rashly made him pope. If one didn't know the man, one might say that in this speech on religious leadership was, in other words, a papal election manifesto.

I do not believe for a moment that it was. Yet Martini stated some basic principles that the next conclave will have to bear in mind. The first is the distinctive nature of religious leadership according to Luke's Gospel: "The kings of the Gentiles exercise lordship over them; and those in authority are called benefactors. But not so with you; rather let the greatest among you become as the youngest, and the leader as one who serves" (Luke 22, 25–26). Religious leadership is, or should be, different in kind, manner, and style from secular leadership. That was what Saint Benedict's Rule said. It is always good to be reminded of that principle. Can one be sure John Paul's pontificate has always avoided that peril?

Cardinal Martini next distinguished three levels of problems that any religious leader has to face. There are internal problems, concerned with, say, lack of vocations or ministers: left-right tensions within the religious community; communication and *koinonia;* "the problem of development (and the distinction between true and false development) and the problems created by resistance to false development, etc." What on earth was he talking about? Various interviews suggest that he was thinking, for example, about birth control or the ordination of married men or women. Martini is not accurately described as a liberal, but he does not regard all questions as settled in advance.

But preoccupation with these internal problems—Martini went on—should not lead the church leader to overlook or ignore the problems thrown up by modern society:

> *War and peace, violence among peoples and groups, defense of human life, abortion, illness, hunger and starvation, the great immigrations, the problem of ecology. Further all the problems of order and tensions in society, especially those connected with the beginning and the end of life, bioethical problems, the tension between technology and ethics, between economics and ethics, etc.*

Well, one might say, anyone can make a list. True. But it helps to have the right list, marking priorities.

The next step is the crucial one. *How* are these contemporary questions to be approached?

> *Contemporary issues are many and in constant movement. It is impossible to have in advance the solution or the right word for all of them. But two things are of the utmost importance.*

To look at these problems as a person of faith, who has in divine Revelation the words and principles for sound action; and to look at them with an eye of comprehension and affection in order to put a human face on problems which are treated by technicians, politicians, and other secular leaders. Religious leaders should always be ready to bring the ethical, moral and faith dimension to public policy issues.

Remember that Martini was here addressing *all* religious leaders, Orthodox and Anglican or Episcopalian as well as Catholic—not to mention, because we were in Jerusalem, rabbis of every stripe. The function of this Jerusalem meeting was to put some content into the concept of "the Judeo-Christian tradition"—an expression that "was not in common use before the twentieth century, and has come to symbolize shared moral values."[6]

But the former Rector of the Gregorian and the Biblicum had not finished. He would no doubt say he was only just beginning. Internal questions and public policy issues may overlap with, but do yet attain to, the true religious dimension. There remain the transcendent problems that are the main specific themes of our religions: "God, salvation, prayer, adoration, faith and hope, forgiveness, life after death, justice and charity and so on. Secular society seems uninterested in these questions. Many people ask from religious leaders answers only about secular problems on the second level." Martini thinks that is a mistaken view:

I do not want to impose my solution to this question. But it is my firm conviction that all people need to face these transcendent problems which belong to the essence of men and women today in this world, even if some secular societies would refrain from publicly putting such questions. . . . We are convinced that these questions are the real vital issues for humanity, and that every other question, no matter how important it appears, depends ultimately on these questions and themes.

Do not misunderstand me. I am not suggesting that Martini was making a bid for the papacy with this Jerusalem speech. It was not conceived as an electoral speech from a promising candidate. But it would serve as a useful draft for the *pro eligendo pontifice* address at the next conclave. Clarity and lucidity are not so common in the Church that we can afford to ignore them when they occur. Martini takes us beyond the conservative-liberal divide—for him a minor internal matter that can be resolved—toward an understanding of what the Church is for.

SIX **Electors as Runners**

This chapter, finally, will look at the electors, who are, by definition, the candidates. Cardinals are made in batches, through an event called a consistory. Pope John Paul II has held six consistories:

date	number of cardinals
June 30, 1979	11
February 2, 1983	16
May 25, 1985	27
June 28, 1988	23
June 28, 1991	22
November 26, 1994	30

Adding up the right-hand list, one finds that John Paul has "created" a grand total of 129 cardinals since 1978. This is a record. However, because many of them were already over eighty when appointed, the maximum number of electors remained 120.

How well do cardinals know each other? A novelty of this pontificate is that it has given the cardinals a chance to get to know one another better than ever before. Hitherto they had met only in consistories and during conclaves. Pope John Paul II brought them together for special meetings as part of his desire "to join them more closely to the pastoral mission of Peter."

There have been five such consultations, on the following themes:

November 4–9, 1979. Wealthy churches to come to the aid of poor ones.

November 23–26, 1982. The "reform" of the Roman Curia and finance. It was a crisis meeting on the latter topic. The press had raised the question of how far the IOR (Institute of Religious Works, commonly, the Vatican Bank) was involved in the crash of the Banco Ambrosiano.

November 20–22, 1985. Immediately preceding the Synod on Vatican II. John Paul II defended the Curia against its critics. Cardinal Ratzinger spoke on primacy and collegiality, and Cardinal Jerôme Hamer on episcopal conferences, which were to be cut down to size.

April 4–6, 1991. Inroads made by the "sects," especially in Latin America. Cardinal Ratzinger announced one authoritative document, possibly an encyclical, on moral questions, and another on the defense of life.

Fixed for May 9–10, 1994, it was postponed to mid-June. How to celebrate the year 2000. An ecumenical meeting of Jews, Christians, and Muslims on Mount Sinai. Repentance for mistakes of the past millennium.

These meetings were unprecedented. To take the college of cardinals thus seriously was, at first blush, an original feature of this pontificate. But it could be considered a rival institution to the synod of bishops established by Pope Paul VI, which was a collegial body in the spirit (and letter) of Vatican II. Present at synods were presidents of episcopal conferences. Many of them were cardinals, but that was not a qualification for the job.

The synods of this pontificate have been six:

1980, On the Role of the Christian Family. Intended by Pope John Paul II as a defense of *Humanae Vitae*, it instead subtly undermined it by calling for a "deeper understanding" of it and an examination of the concept of *intrinsece inhonestum*, which *Humanae Vitae* consciously and deliberately preferred to *Casti Connubii*'s *intrinsece malum*, or intrinsically evil.

1983, Reconciliation and Penance. The aim here was to call into question concepts such as "social sin," which seems to undermine personal sin, and also to manifest opposition to "general absolution," although this was a permissible form of the sacrament of reconciliation foreseen by the reforms of Vatican II.

1985. Called the Extraordinary Synod because it was not in the regular series, its purpose was both to "celebrate" and to qualify Vatican II. Fundamentally it confirmed Vatican II, but it was pessimistic about "the signs of the times" and the collegial reality of episcopal conferences.

1987, The Role of the Laity in the Church and the World. An exciting synod, it involved much participation of the laity in advance in the developed world—none elsewhere.

1990, The Role of the Priest. The principal aim of this synod was to defend clerical celibacy and to oppose requests for the ordination of married men.

1994, The Consecrated Life. A curious title devised so that "secular institutes" could be included along with religious, monks, friars, and nuns. Basil Hume presided. The idea of temporary vows was floated. United States sisters who refused the sacraments from "male priests" were trounced.

True, the *motive* behind these meetings was not to enable the cardinals to get to know one another better. It was to organize their support for the projects of the pontificate.

It involved "delicate" matters such as finance—not to be discussed among consenting adults in public. But from the point of view of this book, the main effect of such meetings was to make the cardinals better informed about the life of the Church. For Cardinal Carlo Maria Martini, archbishop of Milan, this novelty in the history of the Church had greatly strengthened unity:

> There never was such a tangible, strong and—one may say affective—unity. I see this quite clearly in the fraternity and communion among the bishops which flowered at Vatican II and later in the synods. This is a very important "sign of the times" that was not there—or hardly there—in the past. The bishops knew each other then, but not well. Now they visit each other, meet and come together in unity.[1]

Martini was speaking of bishops, but the same applies to cardinals. As he said, they have a chance to meet one another at synods every three years. Observers got into the habit in the pontificate of Paul VI of describing synods as "dress rehearsals for the next conclave." There is still some truth in this description, especially toward the end of a pontificate. In 1994, synods were on Africa and on religious life, and the seriously *papabili* could come to the fore. The Synod on Lebanon lies sometime ahead.

No one, of course, officially "runs" for pope. But there are unofficial ways—lectures, press interviews, and travel— by which a cardinal can discreetly propose his candidature, while denying that anything untoward is being done. Yet obviously cardinals cannot be condemned to Trappist silence, and it would be a grotesque distortion to judge everything they do in the light of a forthcoming conclave that may not happen soon.

With these provisos in mind, I propose in this chapter to look at the leading contenders. It is manifestly impossible, as well as unnecessary, to discuss the chances of every single cardinal elector. But the leading players should be here.

The natural habitat for Curial cardinals is Rome. But they are better observed when they are somewhere else. When they travel they may feel freer; on the other hand, they may sometimes travel as "inspectors" from the head office and be treated accordingly—Cardinal Joseph Ratzinger behaves in this way. Despite his Bavarian smile and love of Mozart, he retains the aura of the Grand Inquisitor. Every September he meets his former doctoral students somewhere in the Alps, halfway between Italy and Germany. Bressanone in Alto Adige (or Sud-Tyrol) is a favorite place. For a week's holiday there is common spiritual endeavor and approximate theological equality. His former students don't have to agree with him. None of them think he is *papabile*.

The cardinal secretary of state, Angelo Sodano, like Chilean wines, does not travel well. He is without doubt the most limited secretary of state of the twentieth century. Compared with his predecessor, Cardinal Agostino Casaroli, whose swan song was his signing of the Treaty of Paris in December 1990, he is a novice who has not yet won respect from the diplomats accredited to the Holy See. His only foreign experience was as nuncio in Chile during the reign of General Augusto Pinochet, whose friend he remains. Sodano is an embarrassment: "a gray man with gray ideas," said one observer.

An astonishing move took Sodano to Santo Domingo in September 1992 to preside over the CELAM (*Consejo Episcopal Latino Americano*) conference of Latin American bishops. He should not have been present at all. The secretary of state should be above intrachurch conflicts. Since the Frenchman Cardinal Jean Villot (1969–79), the first postconciliar secretary of state, his role has been to promote communion among the local churches. By presiding at Santo Domingo, Sodano forfeited any claims to evenhandedness, rashly committed himself on the conservative side, acted as the hatchet man for the Holy Father, and so lost all credibility. He also has a foul temper. At one point, he was so angry with the Latin American bishops that he locked himself in his hotel room and declared his intention of going back to Rome immediately. He was only persuaded to stay by notes pushed under his door. Definitely not *papabile*.

Moreover, there was a curious explanation of why he presided. If one must have a president from the Roman Curia, the "natural" candidate for this post is the prefect of the Congregation of Bishops, who is also, *ex officio*, president of CAL (the Pontifical Commission for Latin America). So the obvious president was Cardinal Bernardin Gantin. But, it was alleged, this French-speaking African who was forced to leave his country of Dahomey (later rebaptized Benin in 1971), didn't have enough Spanish to preside at Santo

Domingo.[2] One is left wondering how, with his defective Spanish, he has contrived to chair all the meetings of CAL since April 8, 1984, when he became its president. A black African president would have been a striking symbol at Santo Domingo. But if he was judged incapable of presiding there, then he will be *a fortiori* incapable of being elected pope.

The CELAM conference was designed as a rally in support of conservative positions. The conservative position, in this context, meant declaring that the five centuries since Christopher Columbus were grounds for unmixed rejoicing. This was certainly the view of Cardinal Nicolás López Rodriguez, archbishop of Santo Domingo and president of CELAM, who organized the celebrations. The event was to be marked by the building of a huge mausoleum, designed to house what the Dominican Republic claimed were the bones of Columbus, and compared by some visitors to a multistory parking garage or an Aztec temple.[3]

Brazilians like Cardinals Paulo Evaristo Arns and Aloisio Lorscheider detested the monument because it represented that alliance of Church and State rejected by most of the Latin American bishops, and even more because over a thousand families had to be evicted from the site to make space for it. Cardinal López Rodriguez denounced critics in the local press as "loudmouths and layabouts." Those who said the Church had something to repent for as well as to celebrate were rudely dismissed as suffering from "a guilt complex that will lessen zeal for the new evangelization."[4]

Cardinal Arns escaped from this stifling atmosphere of special pleading on the first Sunday, celebrating Mass for a crowd gathered beneath the trees of a churchyard. They sang the Nicaraguan *Misa Campesina*, which sees Jesus as carpenter, plumber, and gas station attendant and describes his execution at the hands of "Roman imperialists." At the offertory the people brought up a picture of Archbishop Oscar Romero, a painting of Our Lady of Latin America, and another of a family evicted to make way for the Columbus monument.

The theory that the next pope will come from Latin America overlooks the polarization of the Church there. Those who made the option for the poor—like Arns and Lorscheider, both, incidentally, Franciscans—have been bullied and browbeaten and are too old. They could not rally a majority. The conservatives, on the other hand, are quite simply too nasty and manipulative. Their leader or Roman representative, Cardinal Alfonso Lopez Trujillo (born November 8, 1935), formerly bishop of Medellín in Colombia, wears dark glasses and padded shoulders and has a Mafioso-like appearance.

Yet Lopez Trujillo is worth another look, if only because his rise has been so meteoric that he has been spoken of as a future pope from the early 1980s. As secretary general and later president of CELAM at a very early age, he was very close to Cardinal Sebastiano Baggio, then prefect of the Congregation of Bishops and the sworn enemy of "base communities" and "liberation theology." Ambitious and unscrupulous, he used an eccentric Belgian, Roger Vekemans, who by this time had more contacts with the American CIA than with the Society of Jesus to which he ostensibly belonged. Through the Agency for International Development (AID), a front for the CIA, he channeled over $5 million into anti–liberation theology projects. They also had access to Adveniat funds administered by Franz Hengsbach, bishop of Essen in Germany.

Lopez Trujillo showed his true nature in 1978 as preparations for Puebla were rescheduled for 1979 because of the death of two popes. In his mind the purpose of Puebla would be to reverse the decisions of Medellín in 1968. A vindictive man with a long memory, he said on a tape that by chance fell into the hands of a journalist, "I am convinced that people like [Pedro] Arrupe and [Cardinal Eduardo] Pironio . . . must be told to their faces that they must change their attitude."[5]

Writing to a Brazilian reactionary, Archbishop Luciano Cabral Duarte, he rejoiced in the election of Pope John Paul II because he had spoken "very clearly against the deviations" of liberation theology. He prepared for battle: "Prepare your bomber planes," he wrote, "you must start training the way boxers do before going into the ring for a world championship. May your blows be evangelical and sure."

After that, he was revealed and ceased to be considered as a religious figure. He quarreled with Pax Christi over a report on Central America. In Medellín, he turned the old downtown seminary into a Commercial Center, its beautiful, barrel-vaulted chapel becoming the restaurant. That was in 1982, the very year in which another Medellín citizen, Pablo Escobar, the king of the drug merchants, was elected senator. He paternally helped the poor of Medellín, providing low-cost housing. They turned out in thousands for his funeral on December 3, 1993, after the police had shot him dead.

These connections and revelations would have destroyed a less well-connected man, but Lopez Trujillo enjoyed the favor of Pope John Paul II, who brought him to Rome in 1990 as president of the Council for the Family. Here he has become the ally of Monsignor Carlo Caffarra of the John Paul II Institute for the Family, which is supported by Opus Dei and the Knights of Columbus.

Lopez Trujillo wanted to cut down his fellow Latin American and predecessor as president of CELAM, Argentinian Eduardo Pironio (born December 3, 1920). Paul VI brought him to Rome in 1976 as prefect of the Congregation of Religious. He was a serious Latin American candidate in the two conclaves of 1978. Thereafter his fortunes waned. Sidetracked to the Pontifical Council for the Laity in 1984, he had to surrender effective control of it to the thrusting German bishop Paul Cordes, who had the ear of the pope. Pironio has given up.

One Latin American emerges as a conservative candidate in a pinch: Cardinal Lucas Moreira Neves, O.P. (born September 16, 1925), archbishop of San Salvador da Bahia in Brazil. Before he was appointed to this vast diocese in northeast Brazil in 1987, he had been secretary (that is, effective head) under Cardinal Baggio of the Congregation of Bishops; it was as though, having tried to change the nature of the Brazilian episcopacy from the outside, his mission was to complete the process by joining them.

The best that can be said of him is that since going back home to Brazil his pastoral sense has made him more sympathetic to his fellow Brazilian bishops. An Italian paper has discovered that his maternal grandfather was the son of African slaves,[6] so he has some African blood. The fact that he is a religious must count against him, however, and though there have been Dominican popes before, the example of the inquisitorial Saint Pius V is not encouraging.

Pironio was present and silent at Santo Domingo as part of the huge Vatican delegation that had voting rights. Ratzinger was absent, having hit his head against a radiator in a fall. Other Curial cardinals were out in force. Cardinal Jozef Tomko (born March 11, 1924), is prefect of the Congregation for the Evangelization of Peoples (previously known as Propaganda Fide until Dr. Joseph Goebbels made the word useless). He is a Slovak who bases his position on the fact that Slovakia, now an independent nation, never had an imperialist past. (The same claim was made by his predecessor, Dermot Ryan, former archbishop of Dublin.) Maybe: but Tomko's previous experience in the Congregation for the Doctrine of the Faith suggests that he is essentially an inquisitor.

Cardinal José Sanchez (born March 17, 1920), prefect of the Congregation for the Clergy, has become the chief defender of clerical celibacy. Nothing can faze him—not the statistics of decline, the defection of bishops like Eamon Casey, or Third World demands for a married priesthood on the grounds that "the sacraments are for people" *(sacramenta propter homines)*. The constant debate about the priesthood and its future, he told a conference on celibacy in May 1993, "only goes to show how towering is the figure of the Catholic priest." He does not worry, because "the priesthood enjoys the respect of the great majority of men both within and without the confines of the Church." He seems innocently unaware of the existence of women or rather, like Pope John XXIII in his youth, "strives to behave as though women did not exist."

Eduardo Martinez Somalo (born March 31, 1927), prefect of Religious and Secular Institutes, was briefly substitute, or *sostituto*, and one of the pope's closest aides. A Spaniard and a "friend of Opus Dei," he will join in the Stop Martini movement. As *camerlengo* he will be well placed for that.

Paul Poupard (born August 30, 1930), president of the Council for Culture, which, since 1993, has incorporated the former body for dialogue with unbelievers is an ambitious French intellectual. He served in the Secretariat of State in the pontificate of Paul VI, returning to France as rector of the Institut Catholique.

Roger Etchegaray (born September 22, 1922), president of International Justice and Peace and also of Caritas, is a much more sympathetic Frenchman. He acts as the pope's troubleshooter for the Mediterranean area and has made frequent visits to the former Yugoslavia in a rather desperate attempt to maintain good relations with the Muslims (relative success) and the Serbian Orthodox (relative failure). Previously archbishop of Marseilles, his outlook embraces the whole Mediterranean area. His great boast is that he founded the CCEE (*Concilium Conferentiarum Episcopatum Europearum*, or Council of European Episcopal Conferences).

That completes the cardinals on show at Santo Domingo; practically all the cardinals of Latin America and most of the Curia were present there in October 1991. In September 1993, I was in Prague for the ninth symposium of the CCEE, which could be considered the European equivalent of CELAM.

Prague's baroque setting, miraculously intact, provided an admirable opportunity to study, rub shoulders with, and photograph ten members of the college of cardinals. Ten out of 110—0.9 percent of the electors—a good sample, even if, apart from the curialists, they were all European. Because for the most part they did not know me, they behaved utterly innocently.

I was struck, first of all, by what little contact they had with one another. I began to wonder whether the "effective and affective collegiality" of which the pope so often speaks means anything much. Three French-speakers—Cardinals Jean-Marie Lustiger of Paris, Godfried Danneels of Malines-Brussels, and Basil Hume of Westminster (whose mother was French)—barely greeted one another. It was the journalist, myself, who sat next to the lonely-looking Belgian cardinal on the bus from the airport.

I do not think I saw the next pope in Prague. Danneels (born June 4, 1933) won't quite do. Though he can and does make a good speech as president of Pax Christi, he is the sort of man who comes alive only when he is on a platform. He can be refreshingly blunt. (He declared that *Veritatis Splendor* "is not the best of the encyclicals, but it is an important document.") He lacks human warmth. As professor of liturgy at the Catholic University of Leuven, he had the reputation of a loner who did not communicate with the rest of the faculty. So, sadly for Belgium, which has produced so many fine theologians, he must be crossed off the list.

Danneels has a very critical view of Cardinal Jean-Marie Lustiger (born September 17, 1926), archbishop of Paris. I watched him squirm during the Extraordinary Synod of 1985 as he was forced to listen to Lustiger declaiming his "message to the world," a high-flown and rhetorically ambitious *exercise de style*. Brussels evidently thought that his Parisian brother was altogether too flashy, "too clever by a quarter."

Lustiger is certainly a clever man, and perhaps worth a second thought as pope. The most important things about him are his Polish-Jewish origin and that he had relatives perish at Auschwitz. A Jewish joke asks, "What is the difference between the chief rabbi of France and Cardinal Lustiger?" The answer: "Cardinal Lustiger speaks Yiddish," which draws attention to his Polish connections. His Jewish background would not do him any harm.

But his drawback is that he seems to be entirely a creature of Pope John Paul II, who made him bishop of Orleans in 1979 and archbishop of Paris in 1981. Whether cause or consequence, Lustiger hews close to the papal line. He removed his seminarians from the Institut Catholique in Paris, deeming its theology too "speculative." He sent them instead to the Séminaire Saint Paul in Louvain-la-Neuve, the Jesuit Institut d'Etudes Théologiques in Brussels, or the interdiocesan seminary at Issy-les-Moulineaux—all considered "sounder."

Lustiger is quite consciously trying to form Tridentine priests, men who are essentially set apart for prayer and the sacraments. "He wants," said the Belgian Dominican Philippe Denis, "to be the Monsieur Olier of the twentieth century." On this seventeenth-century model, the priest is *defined* by prayer and the sacraments rather than by mission, by his relationship to God and the hierarchy rather than by his relationship to the people of God.

Lustiger admires the French seventeenth century as "a period of astonishing mysticism." It was indeed. But the effect was to transform the image of Christ the Good Shepherd into Christ the contemplator of the Father. It becomes difficult to see how pastoral and missionary-minded priests can emerge from this process. Lustiger could be considered the candidate of the "charismatic" movement, especially in its French form of the Emmanuel community. He has given their priests charge of the parish of la Trinité, in the ninth arrondissement. Their otherworldly spirit is summed up in their statutes: "To be the brother of Jesus, one must have the Heart of Jesus; and for that one must take Mary into one's household and let the Holy Spirit renew our hearts."

A definite nonrunner is the only cardinal who knows me too well: Basil Hume. Having forbidden me to write his biography, he would prefer to be passed over in silence. At seventy-two (born March 2, 1923) his thoughts are on retirement, during which he hopes to devote himself to fishing at Ampleforth Abbey. Others will have noted, however, his long and successful period as president of the CCEE, in which post he was succeeded by his rather dry friend Cardinal Carlo Maria Martini.

Hume held the post in cold-war days, and no one did more that he did to bring together the two halves of Europe. The "spiritual unity" of Europe proclaimed by Pope John Paul II at Gniezno in June 1979 was translated into reality. "No one side has a monopoly of courage, wisdom or suffering," he said at Ampleforth in 1990. And he repeated the message eloquently in Prague in 1993 and in a recent book, *Remaking Europe*.

Another Anglo-Saxon (as the Latins say) is Cardinal Roger Mahony of Los Angeles. His father was a "full-blooded Canadian-Italian" from Vancouver, who owed his Irish name to the Irish family that adopted him; his mother, Loretta Marie Baron, is a German-American from Ohio. Born in Hollywood on February 27, 1936, he has a twin brother, Louis. He arrived as archbishop in Los Angeles in 1985 and was said to be suffering from two kinds of fever: scarlet fever (for the cardinal's red biretta) and white fever (for the papacy). He, of course, modestly denies that he is "a man who would be pope" and doubts whether any

American citizen of the sole surviving superpower could be considered in a foreseeable future.[7]

However, being "an American" in a diocese as large as Los Angeles, with its 4.5 million Catholics, is less of a limitation than it used to be. Not only does Mahony speak Spanish—he learned it by working alongside Mexican workers on his father's poultry farm—but when installed as archbishop in St. Vibiana's Cathedral he greeted his multiracial diocese not only in English and Spanish but in Vietnamese and Hungarian. And he reads serious theology. In his former classmate Archbishop Justin B. Rigali, secretary of the Congregation of Bishops, he had a hot line to Rome until early in 1994, when Rigali became archbishop of St. Louis.

Mahony was not in Prague. But perhaps there was one runner in Europe's most beautiful baroque city, a silent and observant presence. Cardinal Achille Silvestrini (born October 25, 1923) is a Paul VI man, trained in Vatican diplomacy in the school of Cardinal Agostino Casaroli. Both his interests were summed up in his article on the *Ostpolitik* of Pope Paul VI, in which he revealed for the first time that there was serious planning for a papal visit to Poland in 1966, the millennium year of Polish Christianity.[8]

At first Pope John Paul II seemed not to know what to do with Silvestrini, though he was made a cardinal in 1988. In May 1991 he became prefect of the Congregation for the Oriental Churches in succession to the Indian Simon D. Lourdasamy, who had been out of his depth in the Middle East. Silvestrini took up this poisoned chalice at the most difficult moment—after the Gulf War and with Christians emigrating from Lebanon and elsewhere in droves. His other major responsibility, for the newly legitimate Ukrainian Catholic Church, just up from the underground, was equally nerve-racking.

After only six months in his new post, Silvestrini addressed the Synod on Europe on December 3, 1991. Maybe he did little more than outline the agenda for his office, but that is in itself important, given the ignorance in the West (or in the "Latin" Church) about the Eastern churches in communion with Rome.

Silvestrini echoed Vatican II in stressing that these churches bring a novel and enriching contribution to the life of the universal Church. He listed some elements:

> *The sense of mystery that involves both God's transcendence and "condescension" in the Incarnation; the wretchedness of humankind and the vocation to* theosis *or deification by grace; the constant reference to the Holy Spirit as sanctifier and source of the different* charismata *in the Church; the veneration of the Mother of God, image or icon of the Church, womb of humanity welcoming the Word; the close link between the way of thinking about the Church and the Eucharist (the model of* koinonia *or communion); the ardent expectation of the second coming of Christ.*[9]

Silvestrini did not claim originality for these ideas: indeed, he declared that the "constant teaching of the papal *magisterium*" was that "the patrimony of the oriental churches is an *essential element* in the *fullness* of the Christian tradition."

John Paul II, as a "Latin Slav," appreciates many aspects of the Oriental tradition but is handicapped by his "Polishness," for in Ukraine and Belorussia, where "Latinization" is a live issue, Poles are irremediably perceived as Latin. The same ideas coming from an Italian like Silvestrini might commend themselves. The role of the Oriental churches as a "bridge to the East" would be confirmed. Silvestrini would represent "continuity with an interestingly different style."

He was, however, seventy-one on October 25, 1994, so time is running out. My hunch is that he would make a fine secretary of state rather than a pope. But after a bustling, aggressive papacy, perhaps the cardinals will plump for a more diplomatic and laid-back pontificate.

One of Silvestrini's most attractive features is that he was a genuine "friend of the family" of Federico Fellini, the great fantasist and filmmaker. This became known only when Silvestrini presided at Fellini's funeral Mass in the Roman basilica of Santa Maria degli Angeli on November 3, 1993. It might be said that once dead, Fellini had lost the power to harm. In death he was honored by everyone as a *grande italiano*. But Silvestrini went further. He defined Fellini as "the lord of images," whose poetic power could transform people and everyday realities. That included a savage caricature of the Roman Curia, ridiculed in a fashion parade of disembodied vestments. "It is poetry," Silvestrini went on, "which enters the hearts of the people. We should put our questions to poets, listen to them with devotion, and love them for the knowledge they have of the suffering world."

Fellini criticized the Church, Silvestrini conceded, but always "with irony and with love." His "enjoyment of life" was accompanied by "an affectionate regard for the defenseless and the humble." It was an absolution if not a beatification. It made a great contrast with *Veritatis Splendor*. No one claimed that Fellini was pious, though he was "a Christian in his own way." Actress Giulietta Masina, his wife of fifty years and a devout Catholic, dressed in white "because Federico could not stand mourning." She leaned for support on her brother Mario and clutched her rosary throughout the Requiem Mass. At the end Silvestrini came down and kissed her hands, reverently. Prayers were offered for "this tormented Italy."

And this brings us to the "Italian factor." Italy was "tormented" from 1993 onward because the political system that had prevailed since the war was finally exposed as irremediably corrupt and venal. Various coalitions, usually headed by and always involving the Christian Democratic Party, had ruled without interruption since 1946. The "left," meaning the Communist Party, was excluded as an "alternative" government. The Christian Democrats, with their allies the Socialists (of Bettino Craxi), the Liberals, and the Republicans, were continuously in power. They used patronage and *lotizzazione* (the dividing up of jobs in, for example, national television) to keep things the way they were. They also used bribes. All this was exposed after the collapse of Communism in the Soviet Union and Eastern Europe.

What has this to do with the next conclave? It disqualifies all those Italian cardinals who were so deeply involved with the Christian Democratic Party machine that they can no longer extricate themselves. Whatever the extent of their personal involvement in corruption, they were certainly associated with some of the eight hundred political figures either in prison or awaiting trial. It is no defense for a cardinal to say that "at the time I had simply no idea that my friends were taking bribes and commissions on everything." They should have known.

Unfortunate though all this is for Italy, it simplifies the next conclave. No Italian cardinal stands a chance unless he has spotlessly clean hands. Rome as the capital of Italy inevitably reflects and magnifies the tremors of Italian politics. In 1993 the Italian political system, which had shown remarkable stability since 1946 despite multiple changes of government, collapsed. During the two conclaves of 1978 that stability still prevailed. No longer. If "clean hands" are called for, only two Italian cardinals can pass the test: Carlo Maria Martini of Milan and Silvestrini. And if it is time to return to an Italian after the exciting Polish interlude, and if Martini is excluded as a Jesuit of cautiously liberal views, then Silvestrini stands alone. But he has hinted he will vote for Martini, which is suitably modest of him.

If it is true that "consistories prepare conclaves," then Pope John Paul's consistory in 1991 should give some clues about his mind. When he announced on May 29 that he would be "creating" twenty-two new cardinals on June 28, vigil of the feast of Saints Peter and Paul, he also "revealed" the name of a cardinal already created in 1979 but *in petto* (in his chest—that is, secretly). Ignatius Gong Pinmei was bishop of Shanghai. He served thirty years of a life sentence for "counterrevolutionary activities," and is now, at age eighty-nine, enjoying his retirement in the United States.

So Gong Pinmei will not be at the conclave. But other people who have known the inside of Communist jails will be present: Alexandru Todea (born June 5, 1912), archbishop of Alba Julia, Romania, and the Jesuit Jan Chryzostom Korec (born January 22, 1924), secretly consecrated bishop in 1951 only a year after his priestly ordination. He became bishop of Nitra, Slovakia, in February 1990. Todea is too old; Korec is in the conventional correct age window (sixty-five to seventy years), and he may pick up some East European votes.

Members of the Roman Curia expect a red hat to crown their meritorious careers. Australian Edward Cassidy (born July 5, 1924), in charge of ecumenism, and Pio Laghi (born May 21, 1922), former nuncio to Argentina and the United States, now prefect of the Congregation for Catholic Education, were both honored. Virgilio Noè (born March 30, 1922), sometime papal master of ceremonies, was rewarded, as was Fiorenzo Angelini (born August 1, 1916), responsible for the Vatican's ministry of health workers.

It is sometimes said that becoming a cardinal strengthens one's hand in intracurial fights. Cassidy's hand, in particular, needed strengthening, because ecumenism was slowly drifting into the doldrums. Preoccupied with the impasse in Ukraine, where the Catholics were struggling with three sorts of Orthodox Christians over real estate, Cassidy was reduced to traveling the world talking about the importance of local ecumenism—a sure sign that the "big picture" wasn't playing very well. He had only a minor role in the "welcome" extended to dissident Anglicans who could not stomach women priests and generally, in serious matters, has to play second fiddle to Cardinal Ratzinger.

Henri Schwery (born June 14, 1932) of Sion, Switzerland, was an unusual choice, for the Swiss bishops are so democratic that they have neither primate nor even archbishops; and the presidency rotates.

Latin America got only two new cardinals: the Argentinian Antonio Quarracino (born August 8, 1922), of Buenos Aires, a passionate conservative who flies into towering rages when challenged; and Nicolás López Rodriguez of Santo Domingo, who hosted the pope's visit to his island.

The college was completed with Cahal Daly (born October 1, 1917), archbishop of Armagh and foe of the IRA; Georg Strezinsky (born February 9, 1936), bishop of Berlin; Juan Posadas Ocampo, of Guadalajara (Mexico), later murdered in airport cross fire; Frédéric Etsou-Nzabi-Bamumgwabi (born December 3, 1930), archbishop of Kinshasha, Zaire; and Robert Coffy (born October 24, 1920) of Marseilles. One cannot say they rejuvenated the college of cardinals. The inevitable "joker" in the consistory pack was the ancient Jesuit Paolo Dezza, the man the pope imposed on the Jesuits "to restore order" back in 1981. Almost as old as the century, Dezza won't be at the conclave, which is a pity.

Finally, in announcing this batch of cardinals Pope John Paul declared that there were many other "eminent ecclesiastical personalities, worthy of being elevated to the dignity of cardinal." But he had to stop at 120 cardinals under eighty years old because that was the limit fixed by his predecessor, and he intends to stick to it. So there are limits to papal power; it is not entirely arbitrary; custom and precedent still have a part to play. And in this respect the 265th successor of Peter will be no different from all his predecessors.

SEVEN Preemptive Strikes and Jitters

Marshall McLuhan speaks of a seventeenth-century Boston newspaper that promised to appear twice a week, "or more often if there is a glut of occurrences." There certainly was a glut of occurrences between Easter Sunday, when I handed the publishers the first version of this book, and November 1994, the deadline for this extra chapter for the American edition. Extreme and tough-minded positions were adopted at the Cairo Conference on Population and Development. The papal book *Crossing the Threshold of Hope*, published October 19, certainly crossed all previously known thresholds of hype.

Women were declared definitively unordainable, while the divorced and remarried were to be denied access to the

Eucharist and were advised to live "as brother and sister." It was difficult not to see such measures as preemptive strikes before the pontificate was over.

Yet sycophancy of a high order was expected. Proposition 30 of the Synod on Consecrated Life said that religious should not only "obey the *Magisterium* (or teaching authority) but should welcome it with docility of mind and heart and be grateful for it as a gift of God."[1] But surely, one must first inspect it. The cardinal secretary of state, Angelo Sodano, no less, would not agree, declaring that so far only two popes, Leo and Gregory, had been dubbed "the Great." Now we live in the era of John Paul the Great.

Press officer Joaquín Navarro-Valls continued to display a remarkably resourceful ability to explain away the pope's illnesses. The pope had never been so fit, he explained early in September 1994. The proof was that he read without glasses and showed remarkable powers of concentration for a man of his age. "There was no problem about the pope's *health*," vouchsafed Navarro-Valls as the pope tottered about on two canes on his way to Zagreb on September 11, "only a problem of *mobility*."

In Zagreb, capital of Croatia, John Paul was unable to prostrate himself to kiss the ground; so the turf of Zagreb was raised to his lips on an elegant dish. True, having been raised to the altar by an invisible elevator, John Paul abandoned his canes and greeted the million-strong crowd with expansive gestures north, south, east, and west. But that proved he responded to crowds, not that he was better. In late September his appearance was disconcerting, as his right eye hung permanently puffy and open, while the left eye was closed to a slit.

Dr. Corrado Manni, the papal anesthetist, gave an interview to the *European* in which he reassuringly declared, "The Pope is neither mad nor senile but, in my opinion, he is psychologically unwell." Manni explained:

> *The Holy Father had two operations in 1981, an operation in 1992 to remove a growth, and this year an operation on his shoulder and on his hip. With each operation it becomes more difficult for him to do things, for example walking and climbing, and he becomes more introverted. It is like another bar of the prison going up. All the pleasure of his life has gone, and that is very worrying for his officials.[2]*

It is even more worrying for the Church as a whole and for the college of cardinals. For it heightens the sense of mission of this restless, angst-ridden man. Reduced to unwonted, unwanted, and wholly relative passivity, he feels himself even more "representative" in his sufferings. A tone of mystical exaltation began to course through his words, especially on May 29, which marked his first appearance in public after the hip-replacement operation:

> *This is what Cardinal Wyszynski said to me. I understand I have to lead Christ's Church into the third millennium by prayer, by various programs, but I saw that this is not enough: she must be led by suffering, by the attack thirteen years ago and now by this new sacrifice. Why now, why this year, why in this Year of the Family? Precisely because the*

*family is threatened, because the family is under attack. The
Pope has to be attacked, the Pope has to suffer, so that every
family in the world may see that there is, I would say, a higher
Gospel: the Gospel of suffering by which the future is being prepared, the third millennium of families, of every family and
of all families. . . . Understand it, understand why the Pope
was in hospital again: understand it, think it over.*[3]

This was barely coherent. If the UN's Cairo Conference on
Population and Development were to be approached in
this spirit, then one would have to fear the worst.

In this atmosphere there appeared on the feast of Pentecost, May 22, 1994, an authoritative "apostolic letter,"
Sacerdotalis Ordinatio, signed on his hospital bed. It said
that women could never be ordained as priests. This star-
tled the Catholic world because it seemed to tie the hands
of his successors. How did it come about?

Certain provinces of the Anglican Communion had
been ordaining women since the 1970s, and the Church of
England followed suit with its synod decision of November
11, 1992. Some British Anglicans, especially clergy, felt that
the Church of England had no right to make this decision
on its own and were drawn to cross over to the Catholic
Church. This process was called "swimming the Tiber."

Anxious to rebut the charge that they were hopeless
misogynists leaving the Church of England merely because
of women's ordination, they usually explained that they
were not opposed to the ordination of women "as such" but
were merely declaring a part of the Church did not have

the authority to make such a decision on its own. If the "universal Church" presided over by the Bishop of Rome were to decide to ordain women, then they would be able to accept it.

The position of the Catholic Church on this question had been stated authoritatively by Pope Paul VI in 1976. He was responding to the Anglican ordinations of that time. He ordered a study of the question from various points of view. The Vatican's own Pontifical Biblical Commission concluded by twelve votes to five that "it does not seem that the New Testament alone will permit us to settle in a clear way and once and for all the problem of the possible accession of women to the priesthood."[4]

This no doubt explained the cautious tone of the declaration of the Congregation for the Doctrine of the Faith, *Inter Insigniores*, in 1976. Its key statement was that the Church "does not consider herself authorized to admit women to priestly ordination." That present tense was important. Paul VI was firmly opposed to the ordination of women, but he had a keen sense of precedent; he was unwilling to bind the hands of his successors on this question. A pope should commit himself only where, after careful investigation of all aspects of the question and consultation with the whole Church, he reached an irreformable conclusion. He did not think that process had taken place or that point had been reached.

So theologians felt free to discuss it, knowing that Paul VI was conducting a holding operation, not wishing to settle the question once and for all—that is, "definitively." In any case, the arguments of *Inter Insigniores* proved, on inspection, to be very thin. The Fathers of the Church, when they turned their minds to this question, based their arguments on the inferiority of women. That would no longer do in the twentieth century after *Gaudium et Spes* had said that men and women were "equal but different."

A theologian who was also a cardinal, Carlo Maria Martini, felt able to comment freely as late as April 1993, "The problems, the questions, raised by women's issues, should be taken seriously by *both* sides. Feminism has a tendency to exaggerate its own message, to see everything from one point of view, and no doubt there are good reasons for this. The Church is part of society, and society develops, more rapidly in some sectors than in others." Martini explained that if the Catholic Church were to admit women priests *suddenly*, then there would be a risk of schism, and "the Pope has to be concerned with keeping his huge flock with all its different opinions together."

He went on:

> As for the issue itself, I think we should come to it little by little, to gradual solutions that will satisfy not only the most progressive but also the majority, while remaining true to tradition and also within the bounds of common sense. That's my opinion. But I can foresee decades of struggle ahead. When people ask me, and it's usually Americans: "Will we have women priests?" I answer: "Not in this millennium."[5]

Since there were only seven years to go when Martini made this remark, that could have meant there was not long to wait.

Perhaps it was this interview and others like it that spurred John Paul II on to pronounce. At any rate, he rushed in where Paul VI feared to tread. His encounters with American nuns, nearly all disastrous, provided another motive. Right at the start of his pontificate, during his first visit to the United States, he listened in stony silence as Sister Theresa Kane, then president of the Leadership Conference of Women Religious, urged him "to be mindful of the intense suffering and pain which is part of the life of so many women in these United States." She suggested that the Church's message of human dignity and reverence for the human person required that the Church "respond by providing the possibility of women as persons being included in *all* the ministries of the Church."

Whatever exactly happened—the acoustics were not very good in the Washington shrine of the Immaculate Conception, and some said the pope did not hear these words—this early episode set the scenario for the pontificate. As American sisters became more and more aggressive—as Pope John Paul saw it—so his opposition to them became more and more extreme. They were accused of importing "secular feminism" and "radical feminism" into the Church. Besides, they were threatening to bring these themes to the Synod on the Consecrated Life in autumn 1994. That may explain the timing of the letter.

Moreover, Pope John Paul's personal sense of mission had been enormously strengthened by his illness—as we have seen. Back in the Gemelli Hospital in May 1994, he remembered his first visit there on May 13, 1981, when the bullets of Mehmet Ali Agca could so easily have killed him:

"That shot in St. Peter's Square should have taken the life of the Pope 13 years ago. But instead, the mortal bullet was stopped and the pope lives—lives to serve." It was stopped, he believes, by the hand of Our Lady of Fátima. One bullet remains at the shrine of Fátima in Portugal, and the other at Czestochowa in Poland. They are already relics.

The apostolic letter *Sacerdotalis Ordinatio* is born, then, of a sense of mystical urgency. In chapter 1, I described the malaise in the Church and asked what more remained for the pope to do. Now we know: before it was too late he produced this brief five-page letter designed to commit the Church definitively. Counterarguments are not considered. The letter is an act of authority born of irritation that "in some places the question is considered still open to debate, or that the Church's judgment that women are not to be admitted to ordination . . . has a merely disciplinary force."

So to the crucial passage:

> *Wherefore, in order that all doubt may be removed regarding a matter of great importance, a matter which pertains to the Church's divine constitution itself, in virtue of my ministry of confirming the brethren (cf. Luke 22, 32) I declare that the Church has no authority whatsoever to confer priestly ordination on women and that this judgment is to be definitively held by all the Church's faithful.*

That was clear, peremptory, brutal and decisive.

The question was removed from the realm of theological argument and debate. Where mystical intuition prevails, arguments fade away. Australian Cardinal Edward Cassidy, president of the Council for Christian Unity, explained that the fundamental reason Pope John Paul holds this view is that earth should reflect heaven, where the Redeemer remains for all time a man born of a woman. The glory of women is that a woman was the Mother of the Savior. Holiness matters more than ministry. Paul VI remarked that "the greatest in the kingdom of heaven are not the ministers but the saints," so no affront to the dignity of women is involved in denying them the priestly ministry. It is possible to find this less than utterly convincing.

Some consolation came from the fact that this statement was not "infallible." The grounds for saying this were that it is not presented as such. Formally, that is true, and in such questions the formalities are of the utmost importance. "No doctrine is to be understood as defined," says the 1983 Code of Canon Law, "unless this is manifestly demonstrated" (canon 749, 3). It is certainly arguable that it is not manifestly demonstrated here.

Nor did the pope say he is putting forward this teaching "as Chief Shepherd and Teacher of all Christ's faithful," as canon 749, 1 requires. This teaching does not meet the conditions required for an infallible statement. It is not therefore to be regarded as the second instance of infallible teaching since the declaration of Vatican I in 1870. It is not in the same league as the definition of the Assumption of Our Lady, body and soul, into heaven in 1950.

So there is a tiny gap there. Cardinal Basil Hume, archbishop of Westminster, said, "Although this is not an infallible statement as such, it is nonetheless an authoritative confirmation by the Pope of the position held by the Church on priestly ordination since the time of Christ."

However, some theologians pointed out that although the formal conditions for infallibility were not given, the dominant "Roman school" does not require them. A "note" from the Vatican press office explained that "it is not a question of a new dogmatic formulation but of a doctrine taught by the ordinary *magisterium* in a definitive way." The only way to oppose this is to attack the presuppositions of the Roman school. Hans Küng did this in his 1971 book *Infallible?* So Küng felt free to declare the letter "a disastrous mistake." In this theology, to accept women priests now would be to admit, once again, that "the Holy Spirit was with the Anglican Communion and not with the Catholic Church." The effect is "that the Church's teaching authority has become more and more incredible, something deeply to be deplored."

But bishops and, above all, cardinals, embedded within the Roman system, cannot take this radical option. The best they can hope to do is to engage in damage control. Cardinal Basil Hume pointed to the passage in the letter that says that "the presence and role of women in the life and mission of the Church, although not linked to the ministerial priesthood, remain absolutely necessary and irreplaceable." He pledged himself "to discover and develop further ways of making the role of women even more effective than it already is."

A few weeks later, Cardinal Hume was named as the *relator* or keynote speaker at the October 1994 Synod on the

Consecrated Life. For the first time ever a woman, Sister Emilia Ehrlich, Mother General of the Ursulines of the Roman Union, was made "deputy special secretary" of the synod. The synod resolved that women should take their place in the decision-making bodies of the Church as far as possible. Hume insisted that it was no good saying this unless you explained how it was to be done. The October 1994 synod was not a men versus women contest. Religious men and women stood together shoulder to shoulder in their desire for the universal and international service of the Church. Cardinal Carlo Maria Martini also detected a tiny loophole in the papal letter. "The Pope has said nothing about the ordination of women to the diaconate," he told a Eucharistic Congress in Siena three days after the papal letter, which he accepted as "decisive."

He went on, "But I think our real task when faced with this Letter is not to provide an exegesis from a theological point of view but to see how, despite the difficulties the Letter gives rise to, a path of ecumenical dialogue remains possible, a path in which one can show the presence and mission of women in every field."[6]

One way to do this is to rethink the question of the diaconate for women that certainly existed in the early Church, especially in the East. Martini remarked that it has happened in the past, and can happen again, that a document that "closes down one way may lead to a theological and practical rethinking of another, enabling us to overcome certain difficulties and appreciate better the nature and strength of women in the Church." He concluded: "I think that a certain space remains open." Just how much space is a matter for conjecture. Theologians and canon lawyers will go on discussing the question for decades. But Cardinal Martini's visit to the archbishop of Canterbury and his impressively biblical sermon in Canterbury Cathedral on July 24, 1994, seemed designed to prove that ecumenism was not at a dead end.

Peter Hünermann, professor of theology at Tübingen University and founder-president of the European Society for Catholic Theology, is no knee-jerk dissident, yet he found the biblical basis for *Sacerdotalis Ordinatio* extremely shaky. He argues that the practice of "the Twelve" cannot be normative, for the concept of "apostle" in the New Testament extends far beyond them.[7] In 1 Corinthians 15 Paul says explicitly that after appearing to "Cephas, then to the twelve," Jesus appeared "to more than five hundred brethren at one time, most of whom are still alive, though some have fallen asleep." He adds, "Then he appeared to James, then to *all the apostles*" (15:7). Thus the category of "witnesses to the resurrection" that defines the apostle is much broader than the group of the Twelve. Furthermore, the New Testament prefers to speak of the more fluid concept of "ministry" rather than "ordination," and women were undoubtedly involved in the ministry of the early Church.

How does all this affect the next conclave? The cardinals may wish the pope had stayed his hand, they may complain about the lack of consultation, they may think privately that in old age he has been rambling; but they will rally to his support on the general principle. They have taken an oath of loyalty. They have made a Profession of Faith that includes accepting papal authority.

But they also know what is happening in the Church. They will have perceived the alienation of theologians and the alienation of women. "In the nineteenth century the Church lost the workers," said a Latin American cardinal, "in the twentieth century it is in danger of losing the women."

N B

The next pope will have the difficult task of explaining what his predecessor did not really intend. One could see this process already emerging at the Synod on the Consecrated Life. Thus, after a papacy dedicated to defying and challenging the modern world, the cardinals will have to seek points of reconciliation and harmony. Women may not be priests, but that does not mean that women's ministry does not exist: women are catechists, teachers of their children, spiritual directors, lecturers in theology, possibly deacons.

The statement made in the prelude to this book now comes home with special force: too many voices are excluded from the conclave—the voices of the local churches from four continents, of women, of the young or even the middle-aged, and above all, of the poor all are shut out.

Was that appreciation altered by the nomination of thirty new cardinals, who were created November 26, 1994? Not substantially. Most of the appointments were obvious, being linked to a particular see. The two new American cardinals, Adam J. Maida (born March 18, 1930), archbishop of Detroit, and William Henry Keeler (born March 4, 1931), archbishop of Baltimore, fell into this category. On the other hand, one has to ask why Justin Rigali, since January 1994 archbishop of St. Louis, failed to get his red hat. Maybe he is being groomed to succeed Cardinal John J. O'Connor of New York, who reached retirement age January 15, 1995. There are now ten United States cardinals. A Roman rumor alleges that Pio Laghi, former pro-nuncio in Washington, is "their" candidate. With the naming of thirty more cardinals, the preparations for the conclave are complete. Twenty-three of them were under eighty, so for a brief period at least the college is at full strength and consists of 120 cardinals. The new men are electors rather than candidates. Another consistory (the act by which cardinals are made) will not be necessary or possible unless the pontificate lasts for much longer.

There are six from Communist or ex-Communist countries who will swing the college to the right. Set a man in red to catch a red. Paul Joseph Pham Ding Tung, archbishop of Hanoi, seventy-five, and Jaime Luca Ortega y Alamino, archbishop of Havana, Cuba (born October 18, 1936), will be expected to preside over the disintegration of their regimes.

The two Europeans both have jobs to do. Vinko Puljic (born September 8, 1945), the youngest of the new crop by a decade, owes everything to the fact that he is archbishop of Sarajevo. Once a place of dialogue between Christians and Muslims, it has become a symbol of the failure of dialogue. Miroslav Vlk (pronounced Vilk and meaning "wolf"), born May 17, 1932, is archbishop of Prague, a beautiful, unspoiled city at the heart of Europe.

John Paul II arranged for Vlk, who under the Communists worked as a window cleaner, to oust Martini as president of the CCEE (the European bishops' conference). A simple rule change sufficed: instead of *electing* a special representative to CCEE, chosen on grounds, for example, of linguistic competence, episcopal conference presidents would be *ipso facto* delegates. Italy's president however, Cardinal Camillo Ruini, is not elected by his peers but appointed by the Holy Father.[8] One could speak of the latest batch of cardinals as being part of a Stop Martini campaign.

Jesuit Tom Reese, of the Woodstock Center, Georgetown University, spent 1993–94 in Rome studying the Roman Curia. His view is that the next conclave will be the most difficult and perhaps protracted of modern times. The reason is that this time the cardinals know one another better than ever before: they have watched one another perform, know one another's strengths and weaknesses. They no longer need to rely on the Roman Curia to tell them what to think, as happened in Cardinal Francis J. Spellman's day. In any case, never have Italian cardinals been so few in number: they are down to 18 percent of the total. The 120 cardinals will go into the conclave well aware that they carry with them the voices of young people, of women, and of the poor. These voices are not a distant muffled echo; they are the very heart of the Church. So the college of cardinals, very properly concerned with the credibility of the Church in the modern world, will have to bring in these diverse voices and relay them.

Sacerdotalis Ordinatio conveniently sums up the central weakness of the pontificate. It was an act of the monarchical, or even imperial, papacy produced without serious consultation on its contents or its "opportunity." It showed scant regard for ecumenical implications, declaring, in effect, that in ordaining women the Anglicans had done something that is "impossible." It relied upon obedience rather than persuasion, disciplinary measures rather than explanation. It was scripturally feeble. It treated those who find difficulty accepting it as dissidents. It seemed to threaten a witch-hunt. It reanimated discussion more than it closed it down.

It is time for a new style.

A conclave is a moment of freedom, a chance for the Church to make a fresh start. Conversely, the death of a pope is not a matter for gloom. After all, a pope should be better prepared for death than most of us.

When in 1958 Cardinal Angelo Roncalli heard the news of the death of Pope Pius XII, he wrote in his diary, "Sister death came swiftly and fulfilled her office. . . . One of my favorite phrases brings me great comfort: we are not on earth as museum-keepers, but to cultivate a flourishing garden of life and to prepare a glorious future. The Pope is dead, long live the Pope!"[9]

He did not repine. And neither should we. But it needs an act of faith.

NOTES

Chapter 1

1. Timothy Tindal-Robertson, *Fatima, Russia and Pope John Paul II*, p. 47.

2. The Irish Dominicans, eds. *Religious Life Review*, July-August 1993, pp. 214–15.

3. Pope John Paul II, *Crossing the Threshold of Hope* (Random House, 1994).

4. Ibid., p. 61. In this picture of the world, Jean-Paul Sartre is sitting in the Café de Flore being cuckolded by Simone de Beauvoir.

5. Ibid., p. 34.

6. Patrick du Laubier, *Sociologie de l'Eglise Catholique* (Fribourg: Editions universitaires, 1993), p. 47.

7. Jean Chélini, *Au Vatican de Jean-Paul II* (Paris: Hachette, 1985), p. 279.

8. This formulation comes in Giancarlo Zizola, *Quale Papa?* (Rome: Borla, 1977).

9. See *The Tablet*, June 19, 1993, p. 799.

10. Peter Hebblethwaite, *Introducing John Paul II, the Populist Pope* (Collins, 1982), p. 167.

11. Review of M. Menzo, *Papa Giovanni vescovo di Roma* (Cinisello: Paoline, 1991), in *Cristianesimo nella storia* 14 (1993), p. 92.

Chapter 2

1. de Laubier, *Sociologie de l'Eglise Catholique.*

2. John F. Brodrick, S.J., "The Sacred College of Cardinals, Size and Geographical Composition (1099–1986)," in *Archivum Historiae Pontificiae*, p. 10.

3. Chateaubriand is usually thought of as a conservative thinker because he was opposed to the Enlightenment. But in his preface to *Le Génie du Christianisme* he said that if the book were to be rewritten, he would stress not so much the benefits of religion in the past as "Christianity as the thought of the future and of human freedom." That brought him closer to Lammenais.

4. Margaret Pawley, *Faith and Family: The Life and Circle of Ambrose Philipps de Lisle* (Norwich: Canterbury Press, 1991), p. 42.

5. Pope Pius VII was virtually a prisoner of Napoleon from July 1809 to June 1815. See Paul Claudel's play *l'Otage.*

6. Carlo Falconi, *The Popes in the Twentieth Century* (London: Weidenfeld and Nicolson, 1967), p. 14.

7. Zizola, *Quale Papa?* pp. 135–36.

8. Gerald P. Fogarty, S.J., *The Vatican and the American Hierarchy from 1870 to 1965* (Michael Glazier, 1985), p. 206.

9. Peter Hebblethwaite, *Paul VI: The First Modern Pope*, p. 128.

10. Zizola, *Quale Papa?* p. 138.

11. Fogarty, *The Vatican and the American Hierarchy*, p. 218. O'Connell argued with Cardinal Pietro Gasparri, *camerlengo*, that he should either have given the Americans "some warning of Benedict's failing health or delayed the conclave to give them time to arrive" (p. 219).

12. Hebblethwaite, *Paul VI: The First Modern Pope*, p. 134. This also contains more details on the 1939 conclave. In a footnote on page 133, I said, "Max Bergerre, a young journalist on his first assignment in Rome, found it hard to make out the white smoke against the brilliant sunlight." This got the weather quite wrong. A letter from Denis E. Hurley, emeritus archbishop of Durban, South Africa, put me and the record straight: "The reference is to the thin trail of white smoke that crept from the Sistine chapel chimney. I was in the Piazza that evening and with those around me found it difficult to make out whether the smoke was white or not. To the best of my recollection the reason was that it was already dusk at 5:45 P.M. on the second day of March. I remember commenting that people thousands of miles away from St Peter's knew of the successful election before those of us standing puzzled in the Piazza" (letter of June 22, 1993).

13. Fogarty, *The Vatican and the American Hierarchy*, p. 257.

14. Alberto Melloni, *"Governi e diplomazie davanti all'annuncio del Vaticano II,"* in *A la Veille de Vatican II*, edited by M. Lamberigts and Cl. Soetens (Leuven, 1992), p. 221.

15. Peter Hebblethwaite, *John XXIII: Pope of the Council*, p. 282. A full account is contained in chapter 12, "1958: The Wide-Open Conclave."

16. Loris F. Capovilla, ed., *Lettere ai Familiari*, II, 1968, p. 368.

17. John Cooney, *The American Pope: The Life and Times of Francis Cardinal Spellman* (New York: Times Books, 1984), p. 258.

18. Rome Report, 72, June 6, 1963, unpublished, Canterbury Cathedral Archives.

Chapter 3

1. Giancarlo Zizola, *Microfono di Dio*, p. 232. St. John Lateran is the cathedral church of the Bishop of Rome, and popes lived in the Lateran Palace until 1367 (when they were not in Avignon). St. Peter's belongs to all Christian peoples.

2. Hebblethwaite, *Paul VI*, p. 590.

3. Ibid., p. 591.

4. Zizola, *Quale Papa?*, p. 87.

5. Benny Lai, *Les secrets du Vatican*, p. 172.

6. George A. Schlichte, *Politics in the Purple Kingdom: The Derailment of Vatican II* (Kansas City, MO: Sheed and Ward, 1993), pp. 62–63.

7. Benny Lai, *Il Papa non eletto*, p. 264.

8. John Cornwell, *A Thief in the Night*, p. 265.

9. For this suggestion, see Lai, *Il Papa non eletto*, p. 273.

10. Ibid., p. 278.

11. Ibid., p. 279.

12. Giancarlo Zizola, *Il Conclave: Storia e Segreti* (Newton Compton Editori, 1993), p. 307.

Chapter 4

1. *The Tablet*, October 16, 1993, p. 1356.

2. "Io, il Papa tra l'Ovest e l'Est," *La Stampa*, November 2, 1993; also "States of Savagery, Seeds of Good," *The Guardian*, November 2 1993); also Jas Gawronski, "Jestem Papiezem Zachodu i Wschodu," *Tydodnik Poweszechny* (Universal Weekly), Kraków, November 14, 1993.

3. See René Luneau and Paul Ladrière, eds., in *Le Rêve de Compostelle* (Paris: Centurion, 1989).

4. Giovanni Paolo II, *Europa: un magistero tra storia e profezia*, edited by Mario Spezzibottiani (Milan: Piemme, 1991).

5. Paul Ladrière, p. 153.

6. John Whale, ed., *The Pope from Poland: An Assessment* (London: Collins, 1980), p. 143.

7. Mikhail Gorbachev, *Perestroika* (London: Fontana/Collins, 1987), p. 194.

8. Luneau and Ladrière, eds., *Le Rêve*, pp. 15–16.

9. Address at Ravenna, spring 1986, René Luneau, *Le Rêve*, p. 16.

10. *The Tablet,* December 4, 1993, p. 1599. The Holy See has been a member of the CSCE since it began. It now embraces fifty-seven states and stretches all around the northern hemisphere.

11. Strasbourg, October 11, 1988. In Luneau, *Le Rêve,* p. 28.

12. Quoted in Theo Mechtenberg, "Wie Katholisch ist das Katholische Polen?" in *Orientierung,* February 15, 1993, p. 27.

Chapter 5

1. Halina Bortnowska, *l'Arricchimento della Fede* (Vatican Press, 1981), p. 17.

2. *The Independent Magazine,* October 10, 1993, p. 50. Dawkins is the man who popularized "the selfish gene."

3. *Spectator,* March 5, 1994, p. 27.

4. *New York Times,* August 8. 1993, reviewing my *Paul VI* and David Willey's *God's Politician.*

5. Ladislas Orsy, S.J., "How to Relate Theology and Canon Law," in *Origins* 22 (January 21, 1993). The Hungarian-born Orsy was professor of canon law at The Catholic Univeristy of America.

6. Frank E. Manuel, "Israel and the Enlightenment," in *Religion and America,* p. 61.

Chapter 6

1. Carlo Maria Martini, quoted in "A Pastor's Vision," an interview with Gerard O'Connell, *The Tablet,* July 10, 1993, p. 878.

2. Ignace Berten, O.P., *Santo Domingo 1992,* unpublished mss., p. 6. He remarks that at Medellín in 1968 the two co-presidents were the presidents of CELAM and of CAL; it was the same at Puebla, Mexico, in 1979 when Cardinal Aloisio Lorscheider, president of CELAM, and Cardinal Sebastiano Baggio, president of CAL, were in the chair, but they were joined by the archbishop of Mexico representing local interests. Santo Domingo was an anomaly.

3. See Francis McDonagh, in *The Challenges for the Latin American Church,* Catholic Institute for Internatinal Relations (London, 1993), p. 11.

4. Ibid., p. 14.

5. Penny Lernoux, "Feared Latin Prelate Moving Towards Papacy," *National Catholic Reporter,* September 9, 1993, p. 24.

6. Corrado Incerti, "Manovre cardinale," in *Panorama,* October 21, 1994, p. 25.

7. "Mahony Is a Big Man in the Church," an interview with Arthur Jones, *National Catholic Reporter,* November 12, 1993.

8. Achille Silvestrini, "L'Ostpolitik de Paul VI," in *Notiziario* 20.

9. Achille Silvestrini, "Address to Synod on Europe," December 3, 1991, *Bolletino* 9, p. 7.

Chapter 7

1. The fifty-five propositions are still officially secret. Here is the Latin: "Inter diversa elementa huius communionis ecclesialis efferendum est *obsequium religiosum erga Magisterium,* mentis et cordis docilitate et actione gratiarum quippe quod donum sit Dei."

2. "Suffering of the Pope—By His Doctor," interview with Victoria Streetfield in the *European,* October 7–13, 1994, pp. 1, 3.

3. Translation according to David Remnick, "The Pope in Crisis," *The New Yorker,* October 17, 1994, p. 52. It is interesting that the article was headed "Letter from Vatican City." This was the title used for the four volumes on Vatican II attributed to "Xavier Rynne" (who was in fact Redemptorist Father Francis X. Murphy).

4. "Can Women Be Priests?," in *Origins,* July 1, 1976, pp. 92–96.

5. "The Next Pope?" an interview with John Cornwell in the *Sunday Times Magazine,* April 25, 1993, pp. 22–23. Of course "not in this millennium" could also mean "not for the next thousand years."

6. Carlo Maria Martini, *La Repubblica,* June 3, 1994.

7. See Peter Hebblethwaite, "Ban on Women Priests Is Shaky Conclusion," *National Catholic Reporter,* September 2, 1944, p. 12.

NOTES

The quotation was based on an article in *Herder Korrespondenz*, August, 1994.

    8. I once asked him whether this did not make him feel slightly inferior vis-à-vis other conference presidents. "Not in the slightest," he replied, "for it is a great honor to be chosen by the Holy Father."

    9. Giovanni XXIII, *Quindici Letture*, edited by Loris F. Capovilla (Rome: Storia e letterature, 1970), p. 481.

INDEX